How Much Joy Can You Stand?

How Much Joy Can You Stand?

How to Push Past Your Fears and Create Your Dreams

SUZANNE FALTER

In memory of my father,
John Falter,
and my daughter,
Teal.
They lived with joy.

Contents

How To Use This Book

THIS BOOK WAS WRITTEN in response to that creeping enemy of self-expression: entropy. If you've ever set out to create something, you know what I'm talking about, for sooner or later, no matter how well it's going, the whole damn system breaks down.

The book is organized into short, pungent little essays to read in such moments of flagging enthusiasm. Each essay is intended to inspire and help keep you going, despite the mental sludge.

Keep this book handy wherever you do the work of your dreams, and refer to its pages often. If this book does its job properly, you'll be up and running in no time.

Why Leap Off The Cliff In The First Place?

WHETHER YOU REALIZE IT or not, you and you alone have something unique to create. None of the other billions of other people who populate the earth has your particular talents, knowledge, experience and dreams. This is your birthright – the gift you have been given. Whether it's creating the ultimate bagel, a thriving dry cleaning business, a lifetime of exquisite tapestries, or a child, you are the only one who carries its blueprints.

If you've ever listened to that small, still voice in the dark recesses of your soul, you know this is true. Somewhere in there, the longing to manifest this gift speaks to you on a regular basis; it's that embarrassing dream you keep coming back to, the one that usually feels so hopeless.

The purpose of this book is to explore the one thing necessary to move you towards that dream – your own creative process. This would be the steps you must take to turn your dream into reality. Understanding the sometimes-fickle, sometimes-euphoric nature of all this creating is key to making progress.

So why does there need to be an entire book about your creative process?

Because, if you don't know how it works, you may never realize any of your dreams, whether they are becoming a fine artist, playing pro ball, or managing a mutual fund. Your creative process informs every decision you make, from conceptualizing, problem-solving, and networking, to deciding which emotion to express. And this creativity is not the lone province of artistic types with dirty fingernails and picturesque garrets. Rather, it is a lifeblood we all share – a fundamental human property with millions of applications. It is essential to accomplishing anything in life that's uniquely your own.

Your creative process is the engine that drives your dreams.

Unfortunately, there is one small problem. Out there right now, circulating around the atmosphere, is a carload (an eighteen-wheeler load, really) of out-and-out lies about this process. That would be all the fine excuses we come up with along the way about why we can't make this or that happen. So if you're trying to pursue any kind of dream, you can't help but get run over by them once in a while. Hopefully, armed with enough information and clarity, you can dodge those madly careening trucks and see your way to the other side. I wrote this book in an attempt to prevent further road kill.

I figure all the lies surrounding this process have persisted because we're basically a doubting, disbelieving breed. We have to make up whatever thoughts we can to keep us from doing the work of our dreams, and so the myths persist. In nearly thirty-five years of my own creative work, many of them spent encouraging others to express themselves, I've seen more people cling to more lies that render them absolutely powerless than I ever thought possible. These frustrated creators believe these lies will keep them gloriously afloat, yet such lies are nothing more than leaky life rafts that will only prop them up for a while before giving out entirely. Furthermore, hanging out on a life raft is no substitute for swimming. Whether you admit it or not, that dream of yours isn't going away. Far from it, it will badger you relentlessly until you finally give in and listen.

Chances are your dream has persisted doggedly, and continues to chatter at you regardless of how often you shove it aside. Look at how it reappears at odd, restless times – the middle of the night, or those first crystal clear moments of the day, usually when your mind is free of chatter. The voice of your dream carries on year after year, decade after decade, growing fainter at times and stronger at others, but still refusing to die altogether.

It is almost as if we cannot bear these precious, private visions. The very presence of a dream is incredibly threatening, for to take action and actually follow it requires a freedom we think we do not have – not here, not now, not in this secure, comfort-lined world we've constructed to be as seamless as possible. Pursuing the dream would mean too much hard work, too many demanding hours, less security, less time to chill.

Worst of all, it would mean exposure, and even more mortifying…*potential humiliation.*

Yet, think of how devastating it would be to come to the end of your life and realize you've missed your chance. If you settled for mediocrity, so you must die with most of your potential unrealized. And then you have blown it big time, for there will be no going back.

This withering scenario should never happen at all, for the pursuit of a dream is actually a simple, straightforward affair. Pursuing dreams requires bravery, discipline, patience and ingenuity, yet these are qualities every one of us possesses – *if* we're willing to do the hard work dreams demand. *If* we're willing to honor our creative process instead of fighting it. Pursuing your dreams simply means flexing the muscle of your creativity, slowly at first, but then with more vigor and confidence as you tap more and more into your own passionate conviction and so it becomes stronger and stronger.

Creativity is that magic seed many of us assume we were born without. Yet it is lying latent, waiting in every single one of us. And so this book is about tending that seed, so that it flourishes as effortlessly and as naturally as God, Brahma, the Universe, or whoever originally intended.

Contrary to popular belief, creativity is not a temperamental, whimsical, all-too-fragile breeze that may or may not blow in our direction. This book is intended to smash this myth, as well.

The fact is, your creative instincts are a lot like your underwear; they're right there in the drawer waiting for you to climb into them every day. They're durable and dependable, and they don't play favorites. Your instincts are on call whenever you need them, as long as you remember to reach for them. That really is all you need to know.

Well, okay, you say. But why bother with all this dream-pursuing, creative hoo-ha in the first place?

Simply because of the joy.

If you can manage to leap off the cliff and trust yourself to fly, you will experience a fine, effortless joy like nothing else. You will experience a larger connectedness with the Universe, and possibly for the first time, see your place in it and your own unique value to it. You will be doing what you were always, originally intended to do. This is the secret of the whole process: once you've truly tasted that fantastic fruit of joy, there is literally nothing, not even years of flat out rejection and failure, that can keep you from its magic. The process of creating the dream becomes too pleasurable to resist.

It may take a while to wade through all your resistance, fears, misperceptions, and basic disbelief in yourself – it may take far longer than you think it should. But if you can just keep going through the process, and trust yourself in a basic way not attempted before, the joy will be yours. Your vision and creative instincts will become stronger, clearer, and more vital each time you connect with them. Your commitment will strengthen, and as it does, the world will cooperate in ways you never would have expected. Little signposts will appear along the way, offering support and encouragement. People will show up, bringing challenges, ideas or information. Your dream will begin to materialize, the result of nothing more than finally listening to the still, small voice within and acting accordingly.

It is out of my love for this perfectly simple arrangement that I wrote this book. It is also out of my love for you. The joy is available to all of us, right this minute, here and now, forever and ever.

All you have to ask yourself is this: how much joy can you stand?

🖎 *Try this...*

When the raw stuff of dreams begins to collect, you might want to store it all somewhere. Sprinkle a handful of blank notebooks throughout your life for jotting down ideas and inspirations. Keep a small tape recorder on hand for recording observations. Buy some large plastic boxes for keeping bits and pieces of the raw materials your dream demands. Then designate a specific place for this important cache: the piano bench, an empty closet, or the bottom drawer in your desk.

Once you've begun to collect ideas, materials, odds and ends that pertain to your dream, feel free to dig in to your cache frequently and create. The fact is, the more you write, record, and accumulate, the more power you give to your vision.

Now get out there and have fun.

Dare To Be Heard

SO, YOU WANT TO be a venture capitalist, write a screenplay, or open a Victorian tea garden like the one you visited once in London and never forgot. So, you want to do anything slightly risky that demands a personal vision.

You?...*You?* says the voice, as it collapses on the floor in gales of laughter.

Who do you think you are, anyway?

For many of us, this is where the conversation about pursuing our dream begins and ends. Because, let's admit it – we're sensible people. We're not the sort who takes huge, wild risks. We're not the slightest bit visionary. We don't have a lot of high-minded thoughts that keep us awake at night, and God knows we don't know the first thing those other, more successful people must have known before they set off to realize their dream. We're just...us. Basic. Flawed. Certainly nothing special.

Actually, when you get right down to it, we think we don't really even deserve to have a dream.

Still, we do have this niggling idea that keeps surfacing and resurfacing, begging to be explored, teased out, played with, and realized. We keep having these oddly ambitious stirrings we don't completely understand. So we do what we have always done: we ignore them.

After all, we're just not the kind of people who go off half-cocked after some so-called dream. Right?

The truth is that people with creative impulses need to create, no matter how "uncreative," sensible, logical and otherwise non-impulsive they consider themselves. If we have a pressing idea, we also have an obligation to explore it – and possibly express it. And yet we almost never do. We subscribe to a weirdly common belief that no one wants to hear what we have to say. No one wants to know about our great new idea, patronize a business we might start, attend our would-be productions, or give us any kind of a break. *No one.* We feel as if the world were just waiting to flatten us with some great, universal sledgehammer.

This is the soft, dark underbelly of all dreams, the part that's hovering in the shadows, hoping to derail you. And, this is the first and seediest demon you will have to confront on this path. The really annoying part is that the demon is you. All that supposed rejection is nothing more than your own twisted imaginings. When examined in the cool, rational light of day by other, more benevolent people, your own contribution usually merits a much greater response than you could ever imagine.

I will never forget the first time I performed my cabaret act – a two-woman show in which my partner and I wrote and sang all our own music. For months and months we'd worked on the act, composing, harmonizing, writing lyrics, choreographing moves, all the while convinced that what we were doing was good but strange. At least I believed no one in their right mind was actually going to like this stuff, though we might get some polite applause. In fact, we only kept going because we were having fun.

Then, our opening night rolled around. As we stood on the stage singing our first number, a curious thing happened. People began to smile. They nodded, and sat up a little straighter as if they were actually listening, and then a miracle occurred…they laughed. All of them. Loudly, even. The audience got the first joke in the lyrics, then another, and another. They laughed in places I hadn't even anticipated.

Like some fantastic flying machine lumbering into that sacred moment of lift-off, the act was working. And just then I fully understood the impact of what my partner and I had created and it shocked me.

I was someone worth listening to. People actually wanted to hear what I had to say.

The common disposition among us is a painful sort of shyness. People get embarrassed when called forth to be themself for even a millisecond in front of others. The core belief is that since nothing I say matters to anyone, and so I will end up looking like a dork. This is the precise feeling that keeps people from feeding their dreams.

Oddly enough, that snickering voice of doubt never really goes away. Years go by and you get somewhat used to it, as you learn to test the waters more and more, and eventually the voice slides from an obnoxious bellow into more of a background drone. Witness the famous acceptance speech Sally Fields made on winning her second Oscar: "I guess you really do like me, don't you?" Observe the fact that Truman Capote was once quoted as saying he'd never written anything he thought was *really* good. Not even "Breakfast At Tiffany's." Jane Austen wrote of her work, "I think I may boast to myself to be with all possible vanity, the most unlearned and uninformed female who ever dared to be an authoress."

The point is this: no matter what you take on, insecurity is part of the job description. It's not possible to blaze new trails and forge your own path while remaining on familiar ground. If you want to start a business, you will take on financial risk. If you want to move to another part of the country, you must plunge yourself and whomever is attached to you into the unknown. If you want to try any endeavor you care about, you're going to have to kick it out of that cozy little nook it has carved in your soul. And you're going to have to stand there and watch your dream as it takes its first baby steps towards fulfillment.

This is not an experience for people who crave comfort. Writer Raymond Carver likened publishing his stories to riding at night in the back seat of a driverless car with no lights on.

And yet, such vulnerability can be a valuable part of the creative process. An acting teacher I once knew insisted that serious doubt is actually a very good sign, a signal that you're being completely honest and vulnerable in your work. Mark Twain said of *The Adventures of Huckleberry Finn*, "I like it only tolerably well…and may possibly pigeonhole it [hide it in my desk], or burn the manuscript when it is done." As for me, I only know that I got through the first novel I published by convincing myself no one would ever read it. I was sure that this was yet another little piece of my own personal weirdness that no one would ever have to sit through. And yet, a major publisher actually published it.

Daring to be heard, then, is simple. It's recognizing your cascades of self-doubt for what they are: a whole lot of hot air you've cooked up for absolutely no good reason at all. Then, it's mustering up the courage to trust yourself for five minutes anyway, because maybe you really do have something important to say. And ultimately, it's about saying, "What the hell." Daring to be heard means recognizing that if you put your voice out there, all you're going to get back is a yes or a no. The days of public stoning are long over; so is being pilloried. In fact, a large part of the world won't even be paying attention, no matter how loudly you scream.

Daring to be heard, ultimately, is something great you do for yourself. It's like giving your poor, withered soul some fresh air and sunshine. Daring to be heard means stretching out languorously in the luxury of a strong opinion, or basking in the joy of planning an endeavor you've always wanted to start. No matter what your medium, the dream is yours and yours alone to realize in your own particular way. With the dream comes the chance to represent yourself to the world in a way that truly matters. Daring to be seen and heard becomes your chance for perfect freedom.

It becomes your chance to fly.

✎ *Try this...*

Take a pad of paper and a large, fat magic marker (big, black and permanent works wonderfully well.) Unplug the phone, get family and roommates out of the house, and close your door. Then spend the next half-hour gloriously scrawling out whatever opinion or idea or invective you've wanted to hurl in your life but didn't. Scribble it all out on that pad, as fast and furiously as you can. Don't stop. Don't judge. Don't even think. Just spew. If you run out of paper, get more! Just keep on going until you've said everything you had to say. If you find yourself crying, yelling and pounding the pillows on your bed, all the better.

I find this exercise to be particularly useful after stressful family visits or bad days at work.

How To Get The Fire
In Your Belly

FIRST OF ALL, THE title of this section is deceptive. There really is no "way" to get the fire in your belly about anything, much less the arduous pursuit of a vision. The fire is born through solitary activity requiring not only balls-to-the-wall honesty and extreme patience, but the willingness to chip away for years at work that the world-at-large may never even see.

Passion is an elusive beast, and it appears to land on certain people almost whimsically, through some act of God. This would explain how a 55-year-old New York City doorman I once read about in *The New York Times* was able to put himself through law school at night (a task that included an average of four hours of sleep a night for six years) while the rest of his buddies were content to open doors for other people for the rest of their lives.

The difference between him and the other doormen was not the dream, for you can be sure he wasn't the only guy opening doors for executives in expensive suits and fantasizing about what their lives were like. The difference was that this doorman chose to act. Not only did he choose to act, he chose to do it *no matter what*. That fact that he had to live on next to nothing for years while he paid for his education didn't matter. The fact that he studied until one o'clock every morning, and then got up at five for work didn't matter. The fact that he was the only person in his class with gray hair and middle-aged spread didn't matter. Even the fact that his career would be shortened by his age didn't matter. What mattered to him was one thing: the single and absolute pursuit of his dream. He was going to be a lawyer, *no matter what*.

Not surprisingly, after sending out more than a thousand resumes, he was hired by an associate who was impressed by his tenacity and passion. "I may not get more than ten years from him," this new employer said, "but they're going to be ten excellent years."

What this story has to do with the getting of passion is everything. For passion isn't something one 'gets' at all – it is something one merely allows. That doorman knew he wanted to be a lawyer, and so he stepped out of the way and let his desires take over, no matter how much work that entailed. He didn't doubt, he didn't avoid, he didn't fill the world with a carload of sputtering excuses, and he didn't sweat the details. He merely allowed.

He let the wild, riderless horse of his dream take him on a fantastic ride towards the horizon while he simply surrendered. He listened, he heard, and he said "yes." His willingness was truly stunning.

When I think about passion, I am also reminded of Filomena, a remarkable student I taught once in a continuing ed class about personal essay writing. Filomena was severely disabled with a rare, terminal neuromuscular disease that had left her curled in a wheelchair, only able to write by typing with a stick between her teeth. As life would have it, though, Filomena was the only student in the group of twenty who showed up every single week with her eight pages of essay material faithfully written. Furthermore, not only had she never written creatively before, English was her third language.

What I got from my other students was the usual passel of excuses; what I got from Filomena was the story of her life.

Perhaps it was that this young woman's life was about to end, or maybe it was because most of the time she was housebound in the care of immigrant parents who did not even speak English. Whatever the case, the class became Filomena's confessional, and the pages she wrote were nothing less than the naked truth about how it was to be dying in your mid-twenties. Each week, as we took turns reading her assignments to the class (Filomena's disease had severely affected her ability to speak), the feeling in the room palpably shifted. Here was grace – nothing less than that – and we were fortunate enough to witness it. By the end of the semester, not only were the other students finally gaining enough courage to write, but several had started a support group with Filomena, to encourage her to finish her autobiography before her death.

For each person in the world who pursues her dream, there are hundreds, if not thousands, who only talk about it constantly. Or they think about it constantly. They make lists of great titles for books they could write, or accumulate impressive amounts of sheet music. They stand around at cocktail parties regaling whoever will listen about an idea they have for a novel. Or, they are perennial students who see themselves as having to study well into the next century before they can ever "fully know their craft."

Every one of these people likely has a small, fitfully started, precious piece of work stashed deep in a corner of their closet.

That corner holds an abandoned beginning, evidence of a wonderful moment when their head and heart filled to a point they could no longer bear it; they had to sit down and work. Ideas poured out of them, thoughts congealed wondrously, everything made fantastic sense, and like the March children under the influence of Tinkerbell's magical pixie dust, suddenly they could fly.

Sooner or later, however, struggle arrived. Flush with the false impression that creating would always be so easy, free, and liberating, they expected miracle after miracle each day. Yet, the creative process does not always deliver miracles on cue. They might have been forced to sit and think for a while, and so they might have gotten frustrated. The souls may have sketched out a few ideas they hated, erased them, and drawn up an entire page of ideas they also hated. And then began the slow, toxic spiral down into judgment and shame

So when they finally looked at what they'd accomplished at day's end they had little more than one flimsy page of mediocre work.

"*Proof!* " screamed a voice out of nowhere. "*That's PROOF! You can't do this thing after all...but who are you kidding, anyway? What are you – Leonardo-da-frigging-Vinci or something?*" Enter good old comfortable resignation.

Back to hanging out. Back to the tube and a Bud. In other words, back to reality.

The truth is if you persist into a third day, a fourth day, and a hundredth day, that precious fledgling piece of work might have been nurtured into something great. The creative process is not computer software that provides all the answers at the click of a mouse. Rather, it is a sensitive beast who comes to sit by your side and befriend you only after you've stroked and fed it every day for a good while. This beast demands your care and nurturing. It wants to build up your trust, and it craves your love, because in truth, that beast is only you.

People don't create because they cannot give themselves that critical extra bit of love. They lie terribly to themselves, insisting they can't do it, deciding that they haven't got anything worthwhile to say, pretending that their dreams don't matter. But their dreams do matter. Every unpursued dream leaves the world a tiny bit paler and life a little less rich. Every untold story means one less lesson passed on to someone else. Every abandoned idea means one more strike against hope.

A fire in the belly is a champion for the ridiculous. It keeps you going day after day, stroke after stroke, step after step. You have to keep going, in order to honor yourself. The fire gives you the courage to fly in the face of a world that values products more than people, and the bottom line more than somebody's tender dreams.

The fire in your belly comes only when you're willing to work at your dream for no good reason. You don't pursue the dream because you'll be famous someday, because the work is going to make you rich, or because you'll make better cocktail banter. You design, teach, invent, or serve because this is what you are meant to do.

Getting the fire in the belly means simply surrendering to the truth.

✎ *Try this…*

You have three minutes. Make a list of everything that you are truly passionate about. List anything you can think of, from eating imported chocolate to having great sex to fly-fishing on the Snake River. Then think about what characterizes those experiences. Do you go into a trance and lose track of time? Does the experience leave you feeling you feel like a better, stronger person? How often do you let these passions into your life? Are there any you need to pursue now?

Keep this list and return to it whenever you feel the need to stoke your fire.

Can It Really Be So Simple?

I WOULD LIKE TO suggest something radical.

What if that movie you've always wanted to make, the one you've spent hours silently directing as you chugged home from work on the train and the one you've often fantasized about devoting entire vacations to but still haven't written a word of, was already made?

What if the movie were sitting out there in the Great Beyond, fully formed, just waiting for you to calm down enough to sit down, listen up, and start typing. What would you think?

Initially, you would probably think I am nuts. And yet, I say it is entirely possible.

Inspiration is delightfully unexplainable. The closest any of us can come to naming its source is to say we honestly have no idea. Yet, whenever you get yourself to sit down for a moment and actually listen, something is usually right there in front of you, waiting to be expressed. Of course, the tricky part isn't the expressing, it's the listening.

Often in the past, when I sat down to do something creative, I would hear an absolute cacophony of marching orders:

Okay, smarty pants – think of something. You're not thinking of anything…what's the matter, Stupid?…don't use THAT idea, that's as old as the hills, who wants to hear about that, come up with SOMETHING BETTER…NOW…See? (sigh)…Pitiful.

It was like trying to compose a symphony in the middle of a jack hammering construction site. So no wonder it takes people years to get to the point where they actually sit down and start something.

Meditation helps significantly to quell these critical voices (and we'll talk about that in a later chapter). But you make the single, biggest inroad when you learn to accept the fact that those snarling pitbulls in your head will always be there, on the attack, ready to destroy whatever fragile endeavor you set out to pursue. They will continue to insist what you have designed, planned, or invented isn't really exactly right. They will demand that the project be redone hundreds of times, until your precious creation is as limp and chewed over as a dead dishrag.

Then they will have convinced you that nothing you do, NOTHING, will ever amount to a hill of beans in this world. And it won't…if you listen to them.

First, you have to know these voices for what they are— a mere smokescreen, set up to distract you. A meaningless test, as it were. Then you must simply allow the voices to do their thing and understand that their presence is an integral part of your creative process. Undoubtedly, the voices will blabber on for a while, while you valiantly hang in there, trying to hear the feeble cries of creativity behind all the fracas. Over time, though, the pitbulls will subside. Their protests will gradually grow shorter and shorter, as the voice of your work becomes louder, and you will begin, ever so slowly, to see the value of your undertaking.

So eventually, when you listen, you will hear more and more input that is productive. And while you may be deeply suspicious that creativity could be so simple, you will begin having more fun and so you'll go with it. Fairly soon, you will be able sit down and actually tune out the pitbulls, and tune in the creativity channel directly. And so, finally, you can begin to listen in earnest.

By listening selectively, you will tap into that greatest of all possible teachers: your instinct. While you may study technique, have the help of big-time professors and consultants, and get lots of pointers on how to use your tools, nine-tenths of your creative work still comes directly from your gut. So when you quiet your mind and concentrate hard enough, the guidance is usually there, turning your hand this way and that, moving you to blend unexpected colors. It takes you down alleyway after alleyway, and into the offices of people you'd never expect to meet. It catapults you into entirely unexpected landscapes again and again and again.

All because you've simply learned how to listen.

At such times, this process can feel almost as if you're entering a trance. For when one is truly engaged in any creative act, day-to-day, mundane thoughts melt away as one begins to work. A more powerful force takes over. The simple expression of the soul pours through mind and body as time disappears. Work is completely absorbing. Then you happen to look up and notice three hours have passed, and what you've created is pretty damn great. And that's when you know bliss.

Of course, mistakes are an important part of the process, too. God knows I've gotten it wrong more often than right. Yet, the beautiful thing is that those mistakes are usually guided, too. They're simply part of the creative journey called "my own line of cosmetics" or "some recipes that will eventually be a cookbook." If you surrender to the process fully the mistakes simply become part of the work, prompting you to retackle whatever went wrong until eventually, after extensive reworking, you hit your mark dead on.

I had my own experience of surrendering to the process the first time I ever led a How Much Joy Can You Stand? workshop. A key process involves giving each participant thirty minutes to create something in a completely unconventional way. The pitbulls don't like structures like this, of course, so they swarmed all over my idea protests and sputtering. Still, I persisted as I handed out the materials to the participants. I watched them head off to create, and I felt a pang of fear. As the minutes ticked by, part of me became convinced I'd made a terrible mistake in the midst of an otherwise wonderful workshop.

By the time they returned I was sure I'd ruined everything. But then a little miracle happened. At the appointed hour my group returned…and…they were smiling! Every one of them had something unique and beautiful in hand. Except for one woman, a journalist who'd been suffering from paralyzing writer's block.

"See!" snarled my pitbulls, as I saw the untouched creative material in her hand. *"Just what we thought…. this exercise is for the birds!"*

After the entire group had presented their work, all to much applause, laughter and general celebration, the young journalist got up and hesitantly walked to front of the room with her untouched project – which, in her case, involved a bar of soap.

She stood there silently for a moment while I began to roil in self-doubt. Then, to make matters worse, she began to cry. Finally, the young woman cleared her throat and spoke. "I can't believe you gave me Ivory Soap," she explained, "When I was little my grandmother and I used to make up commercials about it. My grandmother always used to say to me, 'Remember Sari. We are the creative ones in the family. Never be afraid to use your imagination.' " Sari paused and swallowed.

"Now I remember why I have to write," she said.

By this time I was crying, too, as was the rest of the group. And what I finally understood at that moment, in the deepest part of my soul, was that this whole process was guided and all I had to do was trust. And follow the directions.

If you are patient enough, and work and work at your dream, always striving to be utterly faithful to your voice and your path, you will eventually succeed. For you will have brought into being that elusive image you've been carrying around in your head for far too long. You will have given birth to a great, creative wonder, and can now reap the joys of parenthood.

It really IS this simple. The work is out there, waiting for us to heed its call , fall under its spell and bring it into being. Conveying your dream requires only this: your listening heart, give or take nothing.

✎ *Try this...*

If one must have a headful of snarling pitbulls, one might as well schedule them. Pick a time each day when you plan to do your work, and allow the first fifteen minutes strictly for the pitbulls. In other words, schedule your screaming self-doubt right into your work session. Give them lots of room to really raise hell, and try to sit back and observe while they do. You might even write down a few of the more choice ones. Then, once these voices of doubt have had their rant for the day, they should go away and mind their own business, leaving you free to get busy.

The End of Struggle

SOMEWHERE, A LONG TIME ago, someone started a rumor that art, writing and other forms of creative work aren't truly great unless they have been suffered over copiously. Writers should drink heavily, and gnash their teeth when they write. Ballerinas should bleed. Entrepreneurs should spend every last penny they own, and then work like hell while digging themselves deeper into debt. For creativity to be valid, it has to be soaked in fresh struggle.

Balderdash.

What makes a ballet wonderful or a business take off is the simple outpouring of the creator's heart and soul. And, if that person is truly doing his job, that process will involve an immense amount of effort but not a whit of struggle. Effort is the clear-minded application of one's abilities, while struggle is nothing more than a whole lot of unnecessary lather.

It's like this: you decide to open a great little Italian restaurant. You've got your chef lined up, your investors loosely in mind, and you've done the business specs and found that there's a legitimate need in a certain part of town for decent Italian. You've even gone to the extra lengths of getting a few of the old family recipes from your cousin in Naples, and a hot tip on where to buy superb extra virgin olive oil in bulk. So you're off. Every day after your regular job, you start to put in a little time on the restaurant.

Within a few months, two investors are on board, and though you still need a third, you begin to look at rental properties and talk to designers. Day one, day two, day three, day seventy-five pass. You continue to make progress, albeit slowly. Some days go spectacularly; others don't.

Just when you find the fabulous little storefront of your dreams, the one with exposed brick walls and an incredible kitchen, an investor claims he's overextended and drops out. But then another backer miraculously shows up a week later, and he's got a cousin at the Liquor Control Board. You sweat, plan, crunch numbers, and dream. You keep finding recipes and talking to your chef. You're on the verge of signing a lease, when disaster strikes again: your other original investor quits, citing tax problems.

About this time you have lunch with a friend. He asks you how it's going, and you say "Fine, thanks. It's harder than I thought it would be, but I'm getting there." He asks, "How long until you open?" You answer honestly, "Six months, a year. Who knows? I just lost an investor." A worried look passes across your friend's face, and you can feel that quiet reserve of strength suddenly becoming a marshmallow in your gut.

Enter Struggle.

"Bummer," he says with concern. "Yeah, I know," you sigh as you stare at your lunch. Other restaurants seem to spring up overnight, started by people with money to burn – no one is more aware of that than you. Silently, you begin to wonder if maybe this restaurant thing isn't such a great idea to begin with.

At this point you have a choice. You can look at your progress as lousy and something to obsess about, or you can see it as part of a larger process over which you have little or no control. You can choose to mire yourself in struggle…or you can simply forge ahead and open the restaurant anyway.

If you are a struggler, you will begin to brood over whether this project is "really happening" or not. You will doubt; you will stew. In very little time, your mind will become a cluttered mess of conflicting messages with emergency alarms going off all over the place. Meanwhile the once clear and beautiful voice of your project slowly withers away, unable to be heard.

You may stop pursuing the dream at this point, until you realize that this work is a unique creation, unlike any other one you or anyone else has ever attempted, and so it may take a little longer. In fact, your dream may take a *lot* longer. Yet, that's no reason to quit. If anything, it's the reason you need to get right back to work.

The point is this: the work itself does not demand struggle. Your dream demands discipline, honesty, patience, enormous effort, and a fair amount of heart. It demands we give of ourselves or not even bother. And it demands that we love life and people enough that we wish to give back the gift we were given. That is all that your dream requires.

Struggle, on the other hand, is something people bring to the party – one of those base human responses, like the urge to tear open someone else's pile of birthday presents. And ultimately, struggle is really nothing more than a complaint, a way of saying, "I don't want to work this hard. Therefore let me make a major drama out of it and maybe I won't have to."

Basically, struggle is your ego, having its nasty little way.

And actually, when you are truly connected to what you should be doing, struggle is the furthest thing from your mind. All you really want to accomplish is that task set before you, and you'll do pretty much anything to make it happen. Look at Gun and Tom Denhart, who started the children's clothing company Hanna Anderson in their living room. The Denharts' mission was to recreate the high quality, 100% cotton children's clothing from Gun's native Sweden for American consumers. They became so dedicated to communicating the quality of their fabric, that they personally cut and glued tiny one inch squares of the material into 75,000 catalogs themselves. For the Denharts, this was just another labor of love, a natural part of building a business that only eleven years later earned $50 million in revenues.

Struggle is the refuge of people who cannot face their own brilliance.

These are people who, for many reasons, must stay hidden away at all costs. They are the wannabes who sign up for classes diligently, but stop coming halfway through. They're the dabblers who start a million projects, but never finish any of them. Or they're people who simply refuse to stick with anything they care about, and suffer from anorexia of the spirit. And they do this not out of selfishness, but out of old protective wounds designed long ago to keep them safe and small.

Strugglers sorely wish their work to be loved, so much so that they simply can't bear to show it to the world.

Yet, at the same time, struggle should not be confused with the need to take a break. Sometimes, after you've patented sixteen inventions in a row, it might be appropriate to take a few months or even a year off. Yet, still, there is no need for struggle. You can simply realize that the work may not be flowing for a reason – sheer and simple exhaustion. And then you can begin the process of refueling, observing, and allowing yourself plenty of unstructured time to do nothing more than daydream and wonder, which in turn becomes a different sort of creative act.

There is so much sweetness to be found in the disciplined doing of your work. It is an undramatic, everyday sort of life, but so rich and full of pleasure that after a time you cannot *not* do it. What is there for you is simply the uncovering of yourself, an inch at a time; the finer, better part of you who knows no limits, and wishes only to share its own intrinsic genius. This is the part of you that knows the joke about struggle.

It is the strugglers who work hard at struggling; the rest of us work hard at our work.

✎ *Try this…*

Take a pad of paper, and at the top write "Good Reasons Why Not." Then list every single excuse you've used to avoid pursuing your dream. Make sure it's an exhaustive list. Really think about it – take a few days to be certain it's complete. Then put the list away for at least one week.

Schedule a time (and write it in your book) when you will look at this list again. Make sure that you will have no distractions or interruptions when the appointed hour arrives. Sit down with your list, and go through each excuse. Then, with every ounce of honesty you've got, cross out every single excuse that you know in your heart is bogus. Be relentless. The amount of honesty you bring to this step will determine the exercise's effectiveness.

What you will be left with are a handful of items on the list that are your karmic lot in life. If you want to pursue this dream, you'll simply have to deal with them.

On the other hand, you will finally understand that you do, indeed, create your own destiny.

Are You a Drama Junkie?

PERHAPS THE TITLE OF this chapter caught your attention.

I know it struck me when I thought of it. Because in truth, I have observed that so many of us ARE drama junkies – including me.

See if you can relate: you are busy just 'trying to get along'. You do your best to show up fully for your family or friends. You meditate when you can bash your way through to an open spot in your schedule. You honestly do your best to wade through the stuff of life to a little peace.

Life is hard.

And…somehow…you never feel fully in control; everything keeps happening a little too fast. The wild and unexpected seems to keep showing up, derailing everything. You are used to just getting your feet under you…and then all hell breaks loose again. And again. And again.

It's hell, isn't it?

When my 22-year-old daughter died unexpectedly, it

ripped the lid off my pretentions about myself. At the time I was a 'too busy' entrepreneur, 'trying' to get a new business started and doing my best to recover from a tortured, messy break up rife with drama.

A lot of my thoughts were consumed with how injured I was, and how I was going to move forward. Defiantly. Righteously. I was living out of a suitcase and thoughtfully licking my wounds. I had a REALLY good story about why others should take pity on me and give me a soft shoulder to cry on. Lo the drama!

Then the unthinkable happened and my beautiful girl died. And as my mother used to put it, now I REALLY had something to cry about. But here is the truly remarkable thing. Suddenly, I no longer felt like a sad pitiful victim.

Yes, I have done my work over the years…and my propensity for drama was certainly waning. But in this radical situation, the worst thing that can possibly happen to a mother became my salvation.

Teal's death showed me how vastly unimportant my own little stories are…and how profound, rich and abundant my life can be when shared in true service. Now I could see there is only one thing that matters: serving as much transformation as possible to as many as I can reach.

In the days following Teal's unexplainable heart failure, before we had to take her off of life support, my former partner stepped in with support. Quickly we dismissed what had been months of anxiety, upset, 'unfairness' and hurt feelings because now only one thing mattered…Teal and her impending death.

Life was snapped up tight before us, no longer the loose, blowsy meandering path that demanded little of us. Instead, things were tight and intense. The Truth had arrived, white light blazing, and we could see what small, insignificant creatures we had become in its scheme.

All of your drama and mine is nothing more than the mechanics of a childish mind – one that has not yet seen the vast opportunity of this life we have been given.

Did you know that you are brilliant, gifted and profound...but only if you quiet down and tune into that brilliance?

Did you know that you can solve all problems handed to you...but only if you accept that vast, soaring power of yours?

Did you know that you are a sensitive and supreme being who only has to claim your sweet supremacy? For we are ALL born innately supreme – every last one of us. We simply forget to cash in that chip in life, and so we suffer.

Ask yourself this: Is your need to sweat and struggle actually about wanting others to care deeply for you? Is it to prove that you deserve sweet, caring love that seems so hard to give yourself?

To stop the drama, you have to surrender to your own intrinsic ability to heal. And nothing starts that process faster than the admission that you are not your big, tortured story...and that you really can give yourself a break and move on.

Life can be hard at times, it's true. Yet the bigger truth is simple: you are loved and you are Love. That's really all you need to know.

So can you bring it forward in your own heart first?

Can you redirect those impulses that want see each problem as a terrible, life or death Problem.... and instead, see yourself as the Solution?

Can you begin to see the vast opportunity inherent in every left turn?

What belief would you have to give up to do exactly that?

What I know now is that my tortured break up was my path back to self-love. Now I see I was not actually the victim of that messy break up, but the willing co-creator of the drama. I chose that big, fat learning experience 100%, hoping someone else would pick up my sadly broken pieces.

Instead, a beautiful thing happened…I learned to pick up my own pieces. Teal's death was such an extreme yank back to reality that there simply wasn't any other choice.

And so I have become a woman who can take care of herself…without obsessing over my sorry lot. And such is possible for all of us drama junkies.

Perhaps you, too, can dissolve into all that love and joy. When you do, your self-care is deeper, more tender – less about how wounded you are and more about being of service. And your circumstances no longer matter that much. Then you can focus gorgeously on each new gift you have to share.

And then you can truly start to have fun.

Take a look at where life is rubbing you the wrong way right now. Is it really that critical? Or is there some way to shake loose the perception of failure, fear or impending disaster?

For I promise you, you are infinitely capable of dissolving back to the big joy that is your birthright. Right here and right now. All you have to do is allow it in.

Nothing will make God happier.

✎ Try this…

Close your eyes and put your hand on your heart.

Take a few deep, cleansing breaths. Allow yourself to take a moment and connect with yourself, your spiritual guidance, or your sense of the present moment.

Then ask yourself where you have been caught in drama lately. Let the scenes come swimming up to you, one by one.

And as they do allow yourself to note each one as if you are watching a news broadcast.

They are simply pieces of information being given to you. So there is no need to judge, cajole or sink into shame. Just note what is going on.

When the scenes seem complete, thank yourself for providing all that drama...and ask yourself why needed that drama. Let the answer swim up to the surface.

The answer will present itself clearly either now, or at an unexpected moment in a while.

As you complete this process, thank yourself for your willingness to humbly, simply look at what has been...without any added drama. All of it is perfect, blessed and necessary for your growth.

Feel free to make notes and record anything you wish to keep in mind for future reference.

Vulnerability for the Faint of Heart

I AM A PERSON who has never been cool. Although I devoted about three-quarters of my life to the pursuit of cool, it just never gelled. I was always too tall, too awkward, inclined to cry and worst of all, I was constantly being told that my speaking voice sounded exactly like Miss Jane Hathaway's on "The Beverly Hillbillies." I couldn't imagine a less cool person to be compared to.

Somewhere in the vicinity of thirty, I gave up the pursuit of cool. What prompted this was that I finally walked away from a long, fairly tortured relationship. The minute I dredged up enough courage to leave, my entire existence changed. Suddenly, my life went from being about the pursuit of cool to being about the pursuit of nothing. It was as if I had been stripped clean. After all the tears and regrets, all I was left with was my plain, old, unglamorous self.

And so I decided to give this part of me some airtime, simply so I could get to know her better.

Every night after I came home from my job writing toothpaste commercials for a big ad agency, I'd take out a pen and a notebook, sit on the couch and wait. Slowly, the voice of my inner self – that tender, emotional, wiser, more real other person – would begin to express herself. And so I'd find myself making notes. As if by magic, the changes I was going through found their way into words, and these words began to be song lyrics.

Though I'd always sung in an on-again, off-again way, and I'd studied voice for years, I'd never written a song in my life. Yet now I found myself hearing quasi-melodies and rhythms; verses somehow snapped neatly into place. Without knowing how, why, or even what, exactly, was happening, I became a songwriter. Driving those songs was an entire aspect of myself I'd always longed to express but never had.

Eventually, I began to feel the tiniest urge to do something with the stack of songs on my desk. But what? Obviously, I wasn't a *real* songwriter – I was only someone who'd written a few songs that were probably not only terrible, but completely ridiculous. At least, that's what my limited thinking told me.

Still, the small voice within kept on demanding I take them out into the world.

But how? I didn't have melodies for them, so what was I supposed to do? Call up ASCAP and plead my case? Stand on the street with a sign saying "Songwriting Partner Wanted?" I wasn't about to do something serious and official like run an ad on Craig's List (in fact, Craig's List didn't even exist then.) I ended up doing the only thing I could think of: I went to a psychic.

The psychic was amazingly straightforward. "What are all these songs, and why are you hiding them?" she demanded as soon as I walked into the room. She went on to describe a collaborator for me in detail – a tall jazz pianist and composer who was a friend of someone I knew. We would have an uncommonly good vocal blend if we chose to sing together, she said. Three weeks later, I was sitting in the apartment of a tall jazz pianist and composer introduced to me by the friend mentioned in the reading. This woman, a graduate in Composition from the Berklee College of Music, understood my lyrics so completely, and her music for them so achingly beautiful, that the only thing I could do when I heard them was cry.

There I was, the tall, skinny, vulnerable me, written out in chords that expressed something deep and essential I'd always wanted to say. There was the voice I'd been shutting up for all these years, finally given some room to breath. Here was an entirely new and rich way to bring myself forth in the world.

I was amazed, moved, and suddenly filled with passion. My scribblings really were songs after all, and not only that – they were good! Getting the songs out there suddenly became the most important thing in the world to me. It was as if, for the first time, I felt myself to be as completely and fully alive as God intended.

Carey & Falter, the act that our songs turned into, never played Carnegie Hall, but we did play New York's small, back-room cabarets for a wonderful three-year run. For yes, not only could we write great songs – we *did* have an uncommonly beautiful vocal blend, just as the psychic said we would. We developed a small following of core devotees who never missed a show. We lost money and worked our hearts out, practicing for hours every night after our jobs. We infuriated our bosses, confounded our boyfriends and worried our parents, but we couldn't have cared less. For two young, restless women in their twenties, this undertaking became an act of pure and wonderful defiance – a thousand defining moments squeezed into one forty-five minute cabaret act.

What this had to do with vulnerability was everything.

In our own minds, we were flying high without a net. And although neither of us had ever done anything like this, we operated with a weird sort of confidence. It is the same confidence children display when they learn how to ski: they don't think or analyze. They just point the skis down the hill and go, usually in a straight line.

So it was with our act. Whenever a question came up we'd just look at each other and operate on instinct. We were completely and totally in what the Zen Buddhists call 'Beginner Mind.' Because we didn't realize how little we actually knew about creating a cabaret act, we acted with a marvelous, creative certainty that came entirely from our guts.

Furthermore, we were completely passionate about our work, and driven by the delicious freedom of expressing our true selves for a change. There was joy to be found in even the most mundane technical rehearsals and midnight stamp-licking sessions. (This was before the days of social media or even the Internet.) We'd already done the hard part, coming out of our own particular creative closets, so now the rest of our work was painted with the pure and simple happiness of doing what we were truly meant to do.

What we learned was the power of our voices – not just our singing voices, but our *voices*. Our presence. Our essences. We discovered that we had weight in the world and that the simple sharing of ourselves, our true selves, was in and of itself quite moving.

When the author Frank McCourt won the Pulitzer Prize for *Angela's Ashes*, he told *The New York Times*, "I learned the significance of my own insignificant life." It is a shock when you realize the value your own inner secrets hold to others.

Yet, it is true. The public wants to be moved, delighted, and struck by your bravery. They want to see you succeed and they crave your initiative. If you are an artist, people long for the depth of your expression; if you are a businessperson, they hope to be inspired by your vision and creativity. And no, the public doesn't want the canned, corporate version of a good idea – they want *your* good idea, the one that can only come from your own particular set of DNA.

Social Media can teach us something about this. In *The Zen of Social Media Marketing*, author Shama Kabani explains it this way. We are moved by individuals and who they are more than by faceless, anonymous businesses. Think for a moment about which pages you 'like' on Facebook. Wouldn't you rather 'like' your local bagel place as opposed to, say, McDonald's? One is a great reflection on your unique loyalties and values, and where you live, while the other says nothing in particular about you except that you like fast food.

When you think about the great success stories through history, every one of them came about because someone was dreamy enough to think they could actually do something in their own weird way. Consider Benjamin Franklin, Abraham Lincoln, Amelia Earhart and Bill Gates. Lincoln did not free the slaves, and Gates did not start Microsoft because it was the easy thing to do. Franklin did not run around in a rainstorm, hoping to attract lightning for kicks. And Amelia Earhart didn't fly the Atlantic because she was looking for publicity. These people did these things because the small, still voice demanded they must. They succeeded simply because they were unafraid to unabashedly share what they cared about.

These people embraced their own vision, saw the perils, and leapt anyway. They didn't sit around licking their wounds and guarding their most intimate feelings. They probably didn't even consider their feelings or they never would have leapt at all. And they certainly didn't fret over outcomes like being electrocuted or starting a war. Being truly vulnerable means having uncomfortable feelings, facing risks, and barreling ahead anyway. Vulnerability means plunging headfirst into the fear, the uncertainty, and the great stew of the unknown for no good reason other than it's what you have to do. Vulnerability means allowing yourselves to take on the difficult and rise to the occasion, not because you ought to, or because of some guarantee that everything will turn out okay. You assume these challenges simply because you must.

And here is the wonderful pay-off you receive in return: the secret of real vulnerability is that it becomes your greatest source of strength.

Once you're out there in the thick of it, the tender part of you that so feared public excoriation will rise up bigger, better, and stronger, ready to do anything to defend the honor of your endeavor. This is all the support and brilliance you will ever need, unbelievable fortitude, determination, and bravery that seem to come from nowhere. And yet, it will come from you, a natural and powerful aspect of yourself that has always been there, even if previously asleep. Like anything, your vulnerability strengthens with use, melding into your core beliefs about yourself, and feeding your reserves. And slowly, the walls of steel behind it will reveal themselves – walls of steel you probably never even knew you had.

At adventure programs all over the country, people pay large sums of money just so they can tap into these reserves while hanging upside down off a belay line forty feet above ground. Such reserves are real and present in every one of us, yet the only way to reach them is straight through your tenderest parts.

It is not until the beast is unleashed that it can prove its speed, and so it is with the power of your dreams. It is not until you take on risk that you will find out what you are truly made of. And believe me, you're made of far more than you think.

In your vulnerability lies not humiliating goofiness but that divine thread that links us all together. In your vulnerability also lies your power. Simply put, it is where all dreams truly begin.

✎ *Try this…*

Find some old photographs of yourself, preferably from your most awkward, zit-riddled teenage years, or even earlier, when you were still a wild, free little being, full of thoughts and feelings.

Do not choose pictures in which you're smiling politely for the camera. Choose the ones where the camera caught you unguarded and exposed. Choose photographs that remind you of a time and place that mattered deeply to you, an experience that can still stir your emotions when you look at the pictures.

For maximum effect, make oversized copies of the images. Then hang these pictures in the place where you do the work of your dreams.

Where To Look For Inspiration

INSPIRATION IS EVERYWHERE. Most of the time, though, we can't see it. And it isn't even that we don't look; rather, we don't know how to look.

We are living in an era that lacks gratitude. Humor is ironic; disillusionment is the status quo. To wander outside and spend a moment enjoying how softly the snow outlines a sapling is considered a pretty pointless, nerdy thing to do. To be hip, you must be fast, furious, and powered up by the latest technology, whether that's antidepressants or iPads. There is no time for reflection, so don't even bother. "What's it going to get you?" goes the popular thinking.

No small part of our dilemma comes from our addiction to things – smart phones, dumb phones, MacBooks, iPads, laptops, iPods, mini DVD players…the list goes on and on. With them come literally billions of YouTube videos, Facebook updates, Pinterest pins, Instagram photos, videos and podcasts to stream, and the ever-present parade of texts. We are drowning in a world of plug-ins, tools, apps and messages. It's a ceaseless parade of content designed to trap our attention and keep us fixed on our small screen friends no matter where we are.

Yet, these are all ultimately short-sighted technologies that keep us entertained, distracted, totally comfy, and ultimately, utterly bored. They may stimulate our minds, but not our hearts; there is no app for that. Instead, these new technologies provide us with too much stuff to contemplate, and so we contemplate nothing. We sit across the dinner table from our companions – or worse, our children – our faces lit up by the small screen as we let ourselves sink into comfortable distraction.

And so we lose track of each moment as it slides by. We become prisoner to our agendas, another person's tweets, the waited for text that does not arrive. And so we miss much of life. We spend time with others without really connecting. We walk outside to get somewhere, instead of simply taking a walk.

Yet, it is in such simplicity that ideas live. I use to live in Manhattan precisely because I could step out my door and be bombarded with sensations, feelings, spectacles, and insights. Once, someone left an old, upright piano in front of the empty lot across the street from our apartment. In the space of one short day, I saw someone doing t'ai chi beside it in the rain, a very large man doing a Jelly Roll Morton impression for his laughing wife, and a very somber little girl in a Christian Dior coat playing "My Country 'Tis Of Thee." A week later, someone came along and smashed the piano into smithereens with a sledgehammer. The following afternoon, the scrap metal man came and cut off all the strings, and his friend, the scrap lumber man, took the wood. It was the life and death of an abandoned piano, in three short acts. I never could have created this small play so perfectly if I'd tried.

There are tremendous riches around us all the time, but we must tune ourselves into seeing them. Imagine how it is when you live near a mountain. Every time you see it, it seems completely different. Sometimes the mountain is blazing gold, burnished by a brilliant sunset. Other times it is a forbidding block of black on the horizon, and it appears truly menacing. Still other times, the mountain can be the palest lavender, baby pink, or soft gray after a snow; sometimes it disappears altogether in a storm. Our view of the mountain is continuously changing, and one can never predict what it will look like next. From this perspective, the view out your window becomes even better than television for pure, spontaneous entertainment.

The story of Robert Ryman, the artist who pioneered white-on-white, minimalist painting, is a beautiful demonstration of using your environment to fire up your dreams. I knew Ryman when I lived in New York City, and he told me an interesting story about how he began as a painter.

Ryman arrived in New York City in the Fifties, determined to make it as a jazz musician. To make money, he started out as a guard in the Museum of Modern Art, but standing there, day after day, looking at the work on the walls began to get under his skin. At the same time he found himself walking by an art supply store every day on the way to work…soon he found that he was drawn to the materials in an art store. So pretty soon, he took some paint home and began to experiment. And the rest is history.

When you look at Ryman's work today, this all makes perfect sense. For what he does in so much of his painting is make us question the way a piece hangs on the wall, or what its basic components are made of, or even why it exists. His work truly is about art as an idea – an idea you might have plenty of time to consider when standing guard in a great museum hour after hour after hour. For me, this is an ultimate example of finding your inspiration from your everyday surroundings.

The world around us, whether it's the haphazard poetry of city street life or the scattering of autumn leaves in a mountain forest, is the single, greatest creative resource we have. The workings of this world are seemingly random, yet its interplay is fantastically complex and perfect. Whether you believe in spiritual guidance or not, you can't help but find inspiration in the chaos of life. So it is here, in plain, old, boring "everyday" reality, that the best ideas begin. As the old chestnut goes, you've got to use what you know.

To do this, then, begins with gratitude. You've got to perceive of the life that unfolds around you as the rich source of information that it is. You've got to look at the perfect upheavals, coincidences, and crises of your life and the lives around you as what they really are— truly miraculous. You have to cut the stifling back-chatter about "my not-very-interesting existence" and begin to plumb it for raw material. For this is where you will find the solutions to a million different creative problems and possibilities.

You will find a treasure trove of connections and vast networks of supporters. You will uncover stories that have to be told and opportunities that must be seized. Such rich material will not be far away and unreachable, but literally right in front of you.

All that has to be added is your particular take on all this raw material. In fact, this is what makes any creative work great – the presence of you and your feelings in the act of creation. It was Beethoven's massive fury with his growing deafness that made his Ninth Symphony the masterpiece that it is. Edward Hopper was unafraid to convey the loneliness in his own life, as well as in everything around him, which he painted with unflinching dedication. Carolyn McCarthy, who was a registered nurse until her husband and her son were shot on the Long Island Railroad, was unafraid to use her grief to take on gun control laws, which landed her in the House of Representatives.

Each of these people had been committed to one thing: giving us his or her take on the world, as honestly and fully as possible. And that is why their work endures and succeeds, and continues to make an enormous difference today.

The world really does want to know what you think. All you have to do is tell the truth – your truth – in all its glory. If you see unfairness and injustice, then that is what you must express. If you see rage dissolve into sweet forgiveness then that must be your message. If you see a better way to make a mousetrap, then so you must make it. Whatever it is that speaks to you – and stirs your heart – is what you must pass on to others. That is your gift to give back for the simple privilege of being alive.

As Bruce Springsteen once said, "If you're an artist, you try to keep an ear to the ground and an ear to your heart." Well, the same can be said for all of us. Here is where you will find true inspiration.

✎ *Try this…*

Consider putting away your cellphone for a morning, a day or a week. Leave an outgoing message letting people know you have turned it off for a specified amount of time, and that they can contact you by email. Then do not check your email or Facebook more than once during that period, or once daily if you are taking a week long 'media-fast'. If you need support staying away from these platforms, find a friend you can check in with each day who will hold this intention with you. (Perhaps they even join you in this pursuit.)

As you undertake your fast, notice how you feel. You may have to go through a period of withdrawl, especially if you have been heavily dependent on the small screen. And if so, there may be a rough day or two…but I promise on the other side of that you will start to love life in a new, richer, fuller way that is less controlled by how many are contacting you or what's happening with the rest of the world. Instead, quite rightly, the focus will return to you once again…and your dreams.

Make these lists:
- Ten Things I Love About My Life
- Ten Things That Are Uniquely "Me"
- Ten Things I Know That I'd Like to Share
- Ten Things I Could Fix or Change in the World

If You're Looking for Something Else to Do….

Start to collect images of things that are evocative for you by shooting pictures, plumbing old photo albums, and searching through Google images. (Search for the term on Google, then click the word 'Images' in navigation on top.) These want to be images that stir you, inspire you, bring your dream in close. You may even wish to collect quotations, quotation graphics from social media and such. (You can click on any image you see on Facebook and drag it to your desktop or right click to Save As to keep a copy for yourself.)

Put the images in a file on your computer desktop – or print them out and put them on a frequently seen spot in your house. Consider using them as your Facebook cover photo, your desktop image, or even your profile picture in social media. Sprinkle them any place in your life – your bathroom mirror, your refrigerator door, your desk at work – where you can visit them frequently and have your juices stirred a bit.

When you're feeling uninspired and your dream seems dead in the water, take a look at your pictures.

The Luxury of Not Knowing
Your Dream

SOME OF YOU MAY not know yet what your dream is. You may sit silently while your friends go on at length about their plans to start a heli-skiing company in the Andes. You may change the subject when asked directly about your life plans. And you may brood about the fact that you're just not finding "that thing." You may be paralyzed by not being able to say exactly what you want.

I say take heart if you don't know what your dream is yet; you are actually in rich, fertile territory. Furthermore, you have less of a problem than you think you do.

We live in a culture of do-ers – people with big plans and ambitions, and 401K's set up to feed every minute of those dreams. So woe be to those who can't get right out there and start pushing their own personal agenda. And herein lies the problem.

We've been conditioned to think that it's *bad* when we do not know what our dreams are, and that we're *wrong* not to be hard at work already. We think that if we don't know exactly what we want to do in life, we're doomed to failure. How we wish we were like everyone else out there, busily pursuing their dreams. A thick overlay of shame obscures the simple truth that, for better or for worse, we just don't know what we want to do yet.

If we can drop the histrionics and self-criticism for a while, and allow ourselves to simply explore, we can indeed locate those dreams. And we might even have some fun in the process.

Too often we get lulled into thinking that there is only one Perfect Dream out there with our name on it, and no other one will do. Then our minds gnaw away at the possibility that if we do happen to tease out a dream, it's not that perfect one but some half-baked substitute. We assume we're so hopelessly flawed we can't even get our dream right. And we assume that the Perfect Dream is like a whimsical stroke of fortune that may or may not choose to descend upon us. We figure that the Perfect Dream will just find us magically, that we'll wake up one day with a sudden, unexplainable urge to start a B&B in Tahiti, or study rocket science with the mission control guys at NASA.

We forget that we are actually steering the ship.

In truth, there is no Perfect Dream. There are only impulses, some of which lead to major discoveries and successes, others of which lead to nothing,. And still there are others that may only become important later in life. Furthermore, we are the ones who choose to act on those impulses and craft dreams from them. To do that you have to give yourself a whole lot of permission to hear those impulses in the first place. Then you have to give yourself the freedom to explore them with an open heart.

I have learned a lot about this from my friend Bev. Bev appeared in our very small town in upstate New York on a

Saturday in December, having just driven in from Portland, Oregon. She had quit her job as an architect, given up her apartment, left her boyfriend behind, and driven across the country to spend the winter in a small, rented house among strangers in a town of 700 people in the middle of nowhere. All she had was enough savings to last until spring, and some vague plans about doing something with paper or maybe puppetry.

I kept pestering Bev about exactly what she was doing all day. "How are the puppets coming?" I'd ask hopefully. "Oh, I'm not really doing puppets," she'd say. Or she'd look up at me blankly, and then say "I'm actually fooling around with fabric." After a while, it became clear that Bev didn't really know what she was doing, and that she was totally comfortable with that fact. The question was, could I be totally comfortable with that fact?

Bev was doing something radical. As she put it, she was giving herself "the gift of having the freedom to wonder." Unlike most of us, Bev had survived a life threatening form of cancer at age 19. The experience neatly prioritized life for her, so that when the call came to get out there and explore for a while, she was able to muster up the guts to leave her career behind and do it.

Bev has since starred in a play, started a gallery, created art installations with paper sculpture and natural materials, become a successful architect doing big public projects as well as professor of the same. She has traveled down a number of creative roads to pursue exactly what that thing is that she is looking for. Glass blowing has called to her. Puppetry has too, and maybe even writing. To keep the quest going along the way, she took on several different part-time jobs to support herself. Bev continues to live her dream just by having the willingness to try anything and everything that interests her. As she put it to me one day, now she is living life as "the real me."

What I love about this story is the total permission that Bev gave herself. She managed to pry herself loose from the clutches of others' screaming doubts. She managed to change her life in the face of all of her friends demanding to know why – *why why why!!!* – was she doing something so open-ended, vague, and downright strange. Essentially she just allowed herself to do her thing.

And, man, is that rich turf! Because contained within each moment is a secret code to happiness waiting for you to unlock it. And herein you will find all manner of dreams, ideas and food for your soul.

If we feel stuck without a dream, the question we must ask ourselves is what are we not letting ourselves explore? And *why won't we let ourselves explore it?* What is it about the adventure of trying new things that has us so frozen? Is it that we're afraid we won't be brilliant? Or is it that we're afraid we will be brilliant?

Are we worried that if we choose a dream it won't be the 'right' one? Or are we afraid of all those questioning voices around us that demand updates, specifics, and status reports? Do we think we can live with our own harsh critiques and our need to look 'together', polished and professional all the time? Or can we just be authentic, and look like the messy explorers that we are for awhile?

To find your dream you must begin the search, regardless of where it will take you or how it will strike anyone else. You must be willing to give yourself permission to now know – it is this simple lack of permission that has those with no clear dream so hamstrung. For once you stop resisting your own natural, and understandable fears, then you can finally give yourself a break. And then you can start to have fun.

Indeed, some of us were required to avoid our dreams when growing up. It wasn't safe to own key aspects of ourselves – and our tiny, vulnerable child selves struck a bargain…we would let go of those desires in favor of simple survival. It is always life or death in the mind of a child. And so we move towards that which is safe and secure, no matter what is costs us.

But to live your dream, you don't have to suffer unduly. You don't necessarily have to move across the country, nor do you have to quit your job. But you must begin to probe and explore, as Beverly did, for yourself and yourself alone. And if not now, you must ask yourself when.

When *would* be a good time to finally start living your life?

This is the true luxury of not knowing your dream: you begin stripped naked, with no expectations to meet, no mettle to prove, and no agendas to work from. You can be, do and have anything you want. And so you get to bask in the freshness of a new creative undertaking. You get to feel how that project fits inside your own skin. If things work and your project ignites, then…Congratulations! If they don't, then you get to sit back and ponder what might be a better fit. And marvelously .. you get to try again with a lovely, fresh slate.

Your pursuit is not necessarily to find the 'dream', but to track down, step by step, that which feeds your soul and fills your heart. Your mission is to locate that very food you've been hungry for all this time. Once you have tasted even a small bite of it, you will become closer to your purpose on earth. And you will be nurturing yourself as God intended, which always brings a marvelous sense of fullness.

Permission is critical. Can you give yourself permission to fool around with some dreams and see what happens? Can you give yourself the chance to just try something…anything?

Can you give yourself the opportunity, like Beverly did, to live life as "the real you"?

You are worth it, I assure you. No matter what you have done in life until now, the world awaits your gifts. So will you share them, however imperfectly?

🖎 *Try this…*

Create some time when you will be free from interruptions, and then sit back and answer these questions in a notebook. They are designed to give you a toehold as you venture forth in dream territory.

When you were little, what did you want to be when you grew up? Try to write down as many different things as you can.

1. When you got out of school, what were you going to do 'someday'?
2. While waiting in the ATM/checkout/gas station/bank line, occasionally your mind wanders to a great idea. What is it?
3. List five things that you really want to do before you die.
4. Whose permission are you waiting for? (Please be ruthlessly honest.)

There…that should get you started!

The Boring Truth About
Living Your Dream

A COMMON MISPERCEPTION IS that if you want to pursue your dream, you have to know exactly what you're doing all the time. Just look around at all those other more, successful people out there. They move through life with a crisp smile and an unwrinkled shirt, and when you ask them how their work is going they always say the same thing: "Great!"

It's actually kind of nauseating.

The truth is that none of us ever fully knows what we're doing – especially in the diaphanous work of our dreams. We make projections, lists, sketches and plans, but things seldom go as we wish. Unfortunately, life cannot always be planned. It's a fluid, random, ever-changing conglomeration of stuff, people, conditions, attitudes, needs, ideas, and circumstances that careens down the road like an overloaded wagon, ready to overturn at any time. And so you have to be ready to slow down or change tracks at any time, and with that comes your project, trailing intentions.

That's when you wind up by the side of the road, licking your wounds, and cursing your decision to get involved in the whole thing in the first place. And then you remember how little you know. You think about how much all those other people seem to know. Finally, you remember how insecure this whole situation feels. And then…well, hell, why not just quit? Because if you want to make your dream work you have to know what you're doing. Right?

Absolutely, categorically, unequivocally wrong.

The very nature of creating something is that you almost *never* know what you're doing. Sure, you know some technical stuff and you can put together a reasonable looking product. You probably even know most of the steps involved. That's the easy part. But the real meat of the creative process, the inspiration that will set your project on a path of its own, is far more complex and elusive than that.

The popular belief is that inspiration "strikes" us, like a lightning bolt from the sky. Actually, it's the other way around. In reality, we strike inspiration much the way miners strike gold. By ceaselessly working and reworking the old territory, sooner or later we'll run into a little nugget of something wonderful, something better. The more we dig, the more we'll find until – if we're very lucky and very persistent – we hit the motherlode. In reality, creative work is no different from swinging a pick. For every day of incredible divine intervention, there are probably ten spent sifting through the dirt.

This is the bad, boring news about going after what you want: just like any job, there are many times when the work is unexceptional, difficult, and downright demanding. Yet, these are also the days when you hunker down and keep on doing, because there simply isn't any other way to get where you're going. And herein lies the difference between the average dreamer and the person who goes after their dreams. The successful person is willing to put up with the hard work because inside of it she finds a joy like nothing else on earth. But the average dreamer does not know this joy yet. The average dreamer finds his joy in tangible rewards, and gets stopped when he realizes all that hard work may ultimately "be for nothing."

And so your opportunity here is to become the exceptional dreamer...the one who keeps exploring.

When you set out to undertake the work of your dreams, it is critical that you understand something: the reason so many people abandon their fledgling musical comedies, antique stores, and medical careers is because they expected it to be perpetually fun and interesting. "But this is my dream! " they think lustily. "It *has* to be fun." Then the minute the dream gets challenging, which it inevitably does, they quit.

It's as if it suddenly turned into the wrong dream. Or more likely, as if the dreamer decides there is something wrong with him. He imagines he has some weird defect all those other, more successful people never, ever suffer from. In fact, there isn't a thing in the world wrong with anyone who hasn't yet lived his dream. It's just that he doesn't yet understand that pursuing your dream takes effort. *And just because it takes effort is no reason to abandon it.*

Each day spent digging puts you that much closer to the gold. And over time, if you keep at it, a curious thing happens: you begin to love sifting through the dirt. Some of your happiest moments can come during the seventh and eighth rewrites of a novel, when you're reinventing your character's peculiar walk for the umpteenth time. Happiness can be found in the small hours of perpetual sanding you've put in on a fine piece of furniture, when the wood grain begins to be as smooth as silk, and you begin to feel the rightness of what you set out to do. The sanding, itself, becomes your source of joy.

Finally, you can understand all those curious twists and turns you took, and see the larger, greater picture that they form. In the small hours you can finally see the greatness you are capable of creating. This is when all your doubts about your dream begin to blow away, like so much dust in the wind.

This is also the point when you come close to sensing the divine in your work. It does not arrive heralded by trumpet-blowing cherubim, or even in a seamless blast of non-stop inspiration. Rather, the divine steals over you in the small, humdrum hours of your undertaking – during the checking, refining, editing and polishing. The divine creeps in during yet another unexceptional night in your workroom, exactly when you least expect it.

As you climb inside the fantastic nautilus of your creation, you begin to understand why Zen masters spend entire life-times perfecting the tea ceremony. It is the sheer poetry of creating something from nothing, and working on it until it is truly and absolutely right that ultimately keeps you coming back.

This is the magic that can only be born of hard work, and this, ultimately, is realizing your dream.

✏️ *Try this...*

Buy or create an oversized calendar for your dream, then hang it in the space where you do this work. Make a mark on each day that you actively work at your project. You can add qualifying remarks, describing how the work went, or any other notes pertinent to your process. You can go the kiddie-reward route and paste on Superman stickers or gold stars whenever you've pressed through a lot of resistance or managed a breakthrough. Or you can cut out faces from magazines and catalogs and tack them on the calendar to describe the emotional climate of each day's work. You can write one-word descriptions, or stick up summarizing poems or quotations on self-adhesive notes. The important thing is to put a little bit of yourself on that calendar each day that you work at your dream,

Your calendar should be a big, visual journal of the pursuit of your dream; a constant reminder that you are giving yourself an important gift, and that you are, indeed, making progress.

How to Pray and Work
At the Same Time

By NOW, I CAN hear what you're thinking.

Sure, you make it sound easy…but this is NOT going to be easy.

…But I haven't GOT any intuition!

How am I supposed to know what's emotionally honest and what isn't?

But I really HAVEN'T got any time…REALLY!!

HELP!!!!

First of all, remain calm. Or perhaps, more accurately, try to get calm. Calmness is essential to this entire process; calmness, plus trust in that key element, you.

I guarantee that your intuition is there, always has been there, and always will be there. But you're not going to find it until you become still, and learn how to listen. Then, and only then, will you begin to hear your inner guidance and tap into your own vast wellsprings of trust. For me, this has been accomplished a number of ways, the most important being through meditation.

By meditation, I don't mean anything particularly mystical, nor do I mean a "right" way to meditate, as opposed to a "wrong" way. What I mean is methodically stilling the voices in your head for even a few minutes every day – whether it's first thing in the morning, on the train while coming home from work, or when ever you can grab a regular bit of time. Mind you, I've been meditating for thirty years, and it's still a pretty 'difficult' endeavor in that, for me, stillness only seeps in around the edges of my meandering mind. For twenty minutes of meditation, there may only be two or three actual moments of stillness. Still, it seems to work.

Meditation could mean silently counting to yourself as you rhythmically inhale and exhale. It could be methodically emptying your mind of thought again and again as you sit, eyes closed. Checking in your breathing is okay. Noticing the sensations in your body is okay. But that's about it.

Or meditation for you may be finding a mantra, a meaningful little phrase or affirmation that you chant or repeat silently to yourself, or perhaps staring into a mandala or other design, or into the flame from a candle. Meditation could also mean prayer, a walk in the woods, feeding the birds, or having a long, thoughtful run. You must experiment and play with the calming process until you find the combination or the method that is inherently right for you. What is important is the stillness you create, and the regularity with which you do it. At the end of the meditation you want to feel calm, 'empty, grounded and relaxed; almost heavy in your body.

Creativity Meditation

Here is a guided meditation you might consider listening to. If you'd like, you can record the meditation in your own voice and listen to it. Be careful to give yourself plenty of space for pauses.

Begin by sitting in a comfortable position with nothing in your lap. You can be seated in a chair, or on the floor with a cushion, or against the wall. Do not lie down. Close your eyes and begin to breath rhythmically.

Relax your head and your shoulders. Feel the tension drain from your face. Relax your chin and your mouth, and your neck. Breath. Relax your shoulders and the tops of your arms. Feel any tension melt away as you really let go. Breath. Relax your chest and your arms, and let the tension drip out of your fingertips. Relax your belly, and give a sigh. Let your hips go, and relax your buttocks further into your seat. Let go completely.

Relax your legs, your upper thighs, your knees, your calves. Relax your feet and feel any tension you may still have leave completely now, pouring out of your feet into the floor. Let yourself sink into your seat completely and breath.

Now imagine yourself in a beautiful, natural place...a beach, the banks of a river, or a glade in the woods, anyplace that is serene and special. See what is around you and take in all the detail. Smell the smells, and feel the breeze on your skin.

In the distance, see a house. Begin to walk towards it. This is the house where you do the work of your dreams.

There is a path to the door of the house and you take it. When you reach the door, open it and step inside. Notice the entryway around you and the front hall. There is a staircase and you walk to it, and begin to go upstairs. Notice what kind of house this is. Is it lavish and ornate? Simple and rustic? Does it seem like a place of possibility?

Walk up to the second floor and begin to go down the hall. There is a door at the end of the hall and you open it and step inside. This is your studio where you do the work of your dreams. Look around you and notice what materials are in your studio. Are you alone, or is there someone there to help you, like a spirit guide or someone you know?

Go to the place where you do your work and just sit with your work for a few minutes. Then ask your work what it wants you to do next.

Ask your work if there is anything it needs from you to further assist your progress.

Ask your work whom you should ask for help, and where you will find them.

Ask your work for any other help you may need solving particular problems.

Ask your work what else it would like to tell you about your dream.

Ask your work what lessons it is meant to teach your right now.

Allow yourself to feel the full power of divine assistance in your dream, and know that you are truly not alone in this process. Also know that you can go back to this place whenever you wish, for guidance, inspiration, or simply to create. This is the place where you do the work of your dreams, and it exists solely for you.

Feel free to stay as long as you wish. When you feel you have gained all the comfort and insight you need for the moment, prepare to leave. Thank anyone present in the room with you, and thank your dream for its presence in your life. Put the room back to order as it was, and leave it, closing the door behind you. Walk down the hallway, descend the stairs, and head outside.

Begin your walk along the path back to the beautiful spot where you began. Again, notice the sights and smells of this special place and everything about it that you love. Find your way back towards where you began.

When you are ready, move your hands and your feet gently and prepare to open your eyes. You might want to make a few notes about what you learned during your meditation. If things are not clear or obvious now, they will probably become so later.

As you meditate, life itself will become increasingly quiet. The nervousness of the everyday with all its attendant anxieties will subside into the background, subordinate to the great reservoir of calm you are now building at its center. From calmness you will be able to tap into all those lovely creative juices as well as your abundant spiritual connection. The more you plumb the depths of calmness, the greater this resource will become. Ultimately, you will find that the work itself becomes the meditation, putting you directly in touch with your spiritual guidance every time. And so you will naturally do what you do not because it brings home the bacon, but because it has a higher, spiritual purpose. And that is what brings you the joy.

And so you naturally will heed your calling.

I had my own brush with this divinity when I was in my twenties. At the time, I came home from work every night and meditated for an hour or two in an attempt to soothe my work-weary spirits. After a good year of this, I experienced a miracle...and I got one.

I was on a vacation in Scandinavia with my former husband when his back went out. He was lying on the floor of our hotel room on a tiny island in the middle of the Norwegian fjords, groaning and unable to get up. There were no doctors or hospitals or even painkillers around, so I decided to give him a backrub, hoping this might do some good.

Ten minutes into the supposed back rub, my hands began to get extraordinarily hot. Fifteen minutes into it, the back rub had transformed into an energy healing. I could actually feel the pain in Larry's back begin to dissolve and travel up my arms. I was operating completely intuitively, in a semi-trance state I often fell into in my meditations. Somewhere around the twenty-five minute mark, I sat back somewhat groggily and Larry stood up, his back completely healed.

"How did you do that?" he asked, and I honestly had no idea. And so we carried on with our day, and the pain was gone, permanently.

All I could figure was that it had something to do with my desire to help him, and my ability to tap into the great intuitive guidance I'd found through meditating.

Within a month, I seemed to be surrounded by people who needed healing. Then came the day that a friend called who had been stricken with a rash all over her body a few hours before an engagement party in her honor. I went to visit her, and as I laid my hands on her, I felt an overwhelming urge to speak, and so I did, moved by my intuition. My words went on and on, but then stopped abruptly when I had the urge to say that her transition would be signaled by the death of a family pet. Suddenly I felt dubious and afraid. I mean…this detail was *specific*. What if it wasn't accurate?

I was afraid of looking like a fool and I hesitated.

My friend opened her eyes and looked at me. "Go on," she demanded. "What else?"

"Well," I said, drawing in a breath, "the transition will be signaled by the death of a family pet."

Her eyes widened in amazement. "Our dog died this morning," she told me. I'd been completely unaware of this.

I went home and meditated, and told God I would do this healing work, but only if I didn't have to market it. I added that this was not to be a career path for me, but rather an experience of proof. To me, this healing work would serve as proof that I was, indeed, an instrument of God. And that my work was and always would be an expression of that for the rest of my life, no matter how it manifested itself. It was the proof I felt I needed on a conscious level to accept my path.

I discovered this gift because I made room for stillness and Spirit in my life, and I so I continue to do so. I meditate every day because it feels too good not to do it. I literally can not resist its nurturing embrace...the rightness of it. And yes – I don't feel particularly 'good' at it...but perhaps that is not the point.

Once you get in touch with all this lovely, spiritual energy, why not invite it in often – every day, if possible? You can do this through both meditation or prayer and regular work on your dreams. Please notice that I'm not talking about that other, more mundane work you've filled your life with up until now. What I'm talking about is your soul work, the pursuit of which every day – or nearly every day – fills your life with incredible equanimity and joy. Don't just save it for the weekends, stingily doling out crumbs of joy to yourself. Celebrate this gift you have been given – for that's exactly what this bed of desire is.

Like chocolate cake, the more you taste it, the more delicious your dream becomes until, quite literally, you simply can't resist.

It is precisely this deliciousness that leads people to give up their jobs on Wall Street to become sheep farmers, or sell the split-level in suburbia and head off to serve in The Peace Corps. There is a sense of rightness about your dream, and the more you allow this feeling into your life, the stronger it will become. And so you will be led back to a sense rightness that pervades your entire life.

This could be the reason why so many people shake their heads regretfully and mutter, "I could never be that disciplined." What they're really saying is, "I could never allow myself to wake up and hear the calling I've been successfully ignoring for years. I really couldn't stand that much joy."

Hence the title of this book. How much joy can you happily hold in the frame of your life? Can you expand to receive all that God – or your guides – or your intuition – has in store for you? Can you simply tolerate that much happiness?

It's as if we can't bear to be that good to ourselves. It's as if we've always been told to keep it small, and carve out only a modest chunk of satisfaction for ourselves. Whether or not you believe in God, your meditation will serve you by honoring that lost piece of your self. And once honored, that self will not sit silently by. For this reason such regular scheduling of meditation, or of your work, should never be seen as "having discipline," This sounds more like a militaristic police state that makes pursuing your passion sound like...well...grim.

Rather, all I'm suggesting is giving your soul a little space to fool around in every day. And so, that so-called discipline magically turns into freedom. When you do, your soul will sing. Your heart will open. And so you will be reborn.

It is obvious to me that we avoid our creative undertakings simply because we've lost touch with that other, more powerful part of ourselves. We think we haven't got any intuition, or if we do, it's flawed. We think we're too busy to bother listening, we insist there really is no possible space we can work in, or that our toddler, aging mother, needy spouse, or frantic boss is more deserving of every spare minute we have than we are.

Our heads are filled with animated conversations about why we can't stop to feed our passion, instead of why we can. We're convinced that our circumstances are different – *really! Honestly! They ARE!!* We insist that we are special and so we, and we alone, are the only people on the planet none of this applies to. We're convinced there's never enough time, money, or inspiration to do the work, or that there's no point because "none of it will ever see the light of day, anyway." We're convinced no one will give a whit about what we want to contribute.

Most of all, we're convinced that we're right.

What we've forgotten is that this special work of ours is prayer, and I don't necessarily mean the religious version that happens in a church, mosque or temple. Pursuing the dream is the prayer of simply living as we are meant to live. Inherent in this is the understanding that we are not alone, but connected to the pull of the Universe. For it is in our work that we can finally surrender into God's infinite and comforting embrace. Doing our work means realizing that we do not know all the answers, and then relaxing blissfully into our semi-ignorance, simply doing what God has given us to do.

So there is more at stake here than the swing of your moods and whether you'll ever actually get down to work. What pursuing your dream is really about is your place on earth, and the benevolent demands of your own personal version of God.

The world awaits your vision. So when will you find it in yourself to share?

✎ *Try this…*

Begin to walk. I have found a long walk first thing in the morning clears my head and supports my own work incredibly well. And by walking, I mean moving at a brisk pace for at least for at least thirty minutes in comfortable shoes, down a road or around a neighborhood that offers some kind of pleasure. You can take a walk to work, or a meander through a country field; choose the same route again and again, or vary it, depending on your mood.

As you walk, use the time to connect with God, or whomever or whatever you recognize that great big protective force to be. I find myself giving thanks, and having conversations. Sometimes I make up a short affirmation and repeat it in rhythm with my steps. Sometimes I just daydream and as I do fine ideas for my work come along. Whatever the case, I hope you find, as I have, that these spiritual walks feel so wonderful you just can't not do them. (Note: See the bibliography at the back of this book for some books on walks of this type.)

Do this every day or as often as you can. Your work should blossom accordingly.

Expect A Miracle or Two

THERE COMES A MOMENT in the midst of every creative project when the whole damn thing looks impossible. The moment usually arrives when you're on a roll, busily generating ideas, feeling the fun straight down to your toes. It is that terrible moment when you realize you cannot go another step until you've located another half a million bucks by next Friday, or wrangled an hour-long interview with Salman Rushdie on film. Damn your good ideas! What only a moment before seemed like a happening, no-problem project, now, in an instant, has become blatantly impossible.

This is where commitment comes in.

First of all, commitment is not some coat you put on and take off, depending on the weather. It's a promise you make to yourself that must be renewed every single day, and always in the context of work. In other words, you sit down, you do the work, and thereby reaffirm your commitment. If the work has taken a hold of you, you *have* to reaffirm it – it's unavoidable. Thus you will find yourself thinking about your project at odd moments. A bridge for a song might come while waiting in line for a bagel; a sudden solution to a marketing problem might happen in the bath. You find yourself living your project in a most natural, but unexpected way. And in your commitment to it, you find yourself solving the impossible.

Yet, commitment also happens on days when such solutions are not flowing. Then you sit with yourself for a while, computer glowing quietly in front of you, waiting and listening. A few false starts might come along. You'll come up with a few ideas that don't feel particularly connected to anything, so you'll erase them. Then more silence. You might be tired that day, or simply needing a break. And ultimately, you'll take it.

You simply can't solve the problem at this exact moment, but you don't worry. You know your commitment isn't going anywhere; you know you will be back in that chair the next day, waiting and probing for more wonderful stuff. Having an off day does not in any way affect your overall dedication to the project. And this is where the miraculous part comes in: miracles do show up, almost as rewards to your commitment.

One day, while working on a novel, I wrote myself into a corner when I decided one of my characters had to make cream of truffle soup shortly before he killed himself. Now anyone who's been around truffles knows these exotic mushrooms are hard to find, having a season of about fifteen minutes during which they are uprooted by trained pigs, and so they are also hellishly expensive. Still, having never tasted a truffle, I realized I couldn't write about one until I had. The problem was all I had to spend on this particular research was a twenty, even though a healthy bunch of truffles usually cost upwards of a few hundred dollars. Still, off to the local gourmet grocery I went, dubious but willing to try.

I arrived just as the black truffle season was sputtering out, so the person behind the counter offered me white truffles in a jar, in the precise quantity I was looking for. How much, I asked. He inspected the jar. "$23.50," he replied. Amazed and relieved, I told him to wrap them up, which he was doing when his boss appeared and much whispering ensued. The young man seemed crestfallen as the boss walked away. "What happened?" I asked. He looked at me dolefully. "The price was actually $235.00," he said, "but since I quoted you the lower price, that's what you will pay." And while I did feel badly for the young man's misfortune…and I wondered if the difference would come out of his paycheck…a little miracle did indeed come to pass.

Now, I don't mean to get dangerously cosmic here, and suggest that all you have to do is wish for something and it will magically appear on your doorstep. But it is my belief that if your path is straight and true, and you're really listening to your instinct, the world always manages to fall in line with your dream, no matter how outlandish your needs may become.

It is almost as if the world wants us to succeed on our chosen path, and will do whatever is necessary to point us on our way. The story is told that Grandma Moses painted her first large painting because she was wallpapering the living room and ran out of wall paper. Using the brush she'd painted the floor with, she created a quick landscape of butternut trees by a sunny lake, and put it up to cover the gap. An elderly relative loved it and began to encourage her, and so her work as a fine artist began in earnest.

My former husband, Larry, realized his dream of buying a New York City apartment building even though he didn't have nearly the money such a purchase usually demands. He found a building whose price had been slashed twice, since all the tenants were striking and a squatter had taken over the owner's apartment. Everyone he went to for advice told him not to buy the building; a crooked estate lawyer demanded cash in a paper bag just to show it to him. And, he couldn't even get in to see all the apartments because the tenants had changed the locks. Still, after two years of scouring the market, he knew this was the building he wanted, in spite of its many problems.

Larry went ahead and bought the building anyway. As it turned out, the tenants ended their strike after he sat down with them and gave them new leases. And the squatter turned out to be his old girlfriend, a woman he'd been living with a year earlier who'd moved out one day, unannounced, and disappeared. When she found out who her new landlord was, she not only gave up the apartment willingly, but they sat down and had the talk that completed their relationship. And so Larry ended up with the Manhattan apartment building he'd always dreamed of at a price he could afford.

The founder of Sears, Richard W. Sears, began his business while he was employed as a freight processor at the Minneapolis and St. Louis Railroad. One day an unclaimed shipment of watches turned up. After a few weeks, it began gathering dust in the claim room, so the enterprising Sears did a little market research, found out the wholesale costs of the watches, bought the freight himself, and began selling watches up and down the railroad line. This led to his forming the R. W. Sears Watch Company. Interestingly, Mr. Roebuck was the watchmaker who originally did all his watch repairs, so eventually his company took the name Sears, Roebuck & Company.

The point here is that quirks of fate are part of the plan. Complete happenstance, lucky coincidences, and total accidents *do* occur and for good reason. For I believe such occurrences aren't really accidents at all, but traffic signs pointing the way. They happen almost as rewards to your single-minded dedication to your project, showing up to affirm your path, and to give you that little goose of encouragement you need.

Now I know someone somewhere is reading this right now saying, "I decide I need half a million in funding and it will just magically show up in front of me. Yeah, right!"

All I have to say to that is bend your imagination a little. So what if this is only my opinion, and not some scientifically proven fact? Such thinking can only help you with your own particular vision. One of the things I love most about life is what a mystery the human brain is. The truth is, we really don't have any idea how these so-called coincidences occur – whether we have some sort of extra sensory skills that can predetermine them, or whether they really are acts of God, or completely without meaning.

The key is to receive such synergy as a gift, for if nothing else, it will provide critical ballast the next time your impetus begins to sag. "Hold fast to your dreams," said Walt Whitman.

And while you're at it, expect a few miracles, say I.

✎ *Try this…*

Before you decide you're one of those people for whom miracles never happen, pull out your journal or your notebook. Then make a list of miracles that have happened in your life – unexpected twists of fate and chance encounters that led to important relationships and opportunities. Think hard about what you'd set out to do when your miracle occurred. Record all the details: what you thought was going to happen, what actually did happen, where this led you, and any other outcomes you can think of.

You might be surprised to find you've experienced more miracles than you ever thought possible.

Now make a new list: the miracles you want to have happen. Feel free to be as fantastic as you like in assembling this list – write down even the miracles that you think have *no chance* of occurring. (Be careful you're not just coming up with any old miracle, but choose the ones that really seem right for you and your cause.)

Then tuck that list away in a drawer or a file and forget about it. Don't be surprised if some of them do, indeed, come true.

Why Geniuses Have Genius

As far as I can tell, true genius is a fairly simple affair. What geniuses do is recognize their gifts, and then fully and completely embrace their craft.

By this I mean that they live it, twenty-four hours a day, for most of their adult life. The stories abound. The English painter Lucien Freud rarely left his London studio, except to visit the National Museum during his favorite off-hours, between 11 PM and 5 AM. The great soprano Marilyn Horne once told a Sixty Minutes interviewer that she does not speak while on tour, not even a word, until each night's concert has been given. The painter Andrew Wyeth never wore a watch for fear that any sort of schedule would interrupt the flow of his painting. Stevie Wonder is known to travel with a keyboard everywhere he goes, so an assistant can set it up. As documented in a profile in The New Yorker, Wonder would break off mid-sentence to step off and compose for a while…no matter what else was going on. He simply had to stay in the flow.

And so it is.

These people achieved success because they gave themselves over fully and completely to their passion. Their first and utmost priority in their life was or is their work, and they went there without question. Long ago, they passed the threshold where one is controlled by doubt and hesitation. Their work is the love of their life, a pull they are physically unable to resist.

This is how Matisse entered the final, most incredible phase of his career as an invalid, creating masterpieces of color and simplicity from his sickbed. This is how Michelangelo created the David, working inside wooden walls he constructed around the eighteen-foot-high block of marble. He stayed there for days on end, sleeping in his clothing, stopping only for occasional bread and water, even working by torchlight at night. What the genius knows is out-and-out surrender to his creativity.

Once success begins, the issue of responsibility also emerges. Some geniuses keep creating on a certain level because it is expected of them, but others recognize the sacredness of the creative process, and remain authentic to its call. Consider the Nobel Prize winning Japanese novelist, Kenzaburo Oe, who quit writing fiction at the height of his popularity in Japan and around the world. Oe, who wrote almost exclusively about his brain-damaged son in his novels, felt he'd said everything he had to say in his fiction. And so he stopped, with the same bravery and total respect for honesty that had made him a success in the first place.

Similar stories are told about the legendary airplane designer Clarence L. "Kelly" Johnson, who founded Lockheed's underground technology think tank, The Skunk Works. In one instance, Johnson returned millions of dollars to the Air Force after deciding his team could not build a hydrogen-powered plane. He did this freely, despite the considerable financial loss such a move meant for Lockheed.

A genius will always surrender to all the emotional demands of his work, no matter how frightening or challenging they may be, even if they invite public excoriation. Orson Welles will always be considered a genius, and Citizen Kane will always be one of the great movies of all time, but not because either was polite or well-liked. In fact, Citizen Kane (a scathing, thinly-veiled portrayal of William Randolph Hearst and his mistress, Marion Davies) was screened only briefly after it was made, and won only one Oscar (for best screenplay.) The movie was hidden away in the RKO vault for more than a decade because the studio was afraid to release it widely because of its controversial subject matter.

Welles, himself, was openly booed at the 1941 Oscars each time his name was mentioned, and retained semi-pariah status for the rest of his career. Yet when you look at Citizen Kane even today, it is almost overpowering in its freshness. Indeed, its considered one of the greatest movies every made. It remains a unique, hauntingly honest portrait of a character who, like the best of Shakespeare, simply refuses to go away.

The treatment of geniuses is the same throughout history. The Impressionist movement began in a tent outside the Academy in Paris, bearing a sign, "Salon des Refusees", or, Exhibit of the Rejects. This is how Manet, Monet, Renoir and Degas first showed their vision to the world, after Academy officials refused to exhibit their work. Parisian crowds laughed at the paintings, and were particularly scandalized by Manet's "Olympia," a portrait of a common woman, most likely a prostitute, painted utterly realistically to mock the Academy's neo-Classical "divine maidens." In fact, "Olympia" had to be hung high, so to be kept safe from being attacked by the walking sticks and umbrellas of outraged viewers. Yet, today, these works are among the most beloved of all paintings, while Neo-Classicism long ago stopped drawing huge crowds.

Genius is brash and audacious. It feels its own relevance — and smashes convention with delight and refuses to be ignored. It defies the social animal in all of us that's trained to be polite, clever, and adorable, and chooses the path of raw veracity every time. Genius exists for itself and the sheer joy of its release into the world, and yet it exists for us, as well. For we need its power and its roughness, just as we need the tranquility of the everyday.

Geniuses have genius because they simply have no choice. Their gift is prodigious enough that they won't have a moment's peace until they have ridden its wild horses straight into the sun. All of us, in fact, have a touch of this genius. Whether our gift is baking bread, assessing environmental hazards, teaching children, or powerhouse investing. And we know its truth: it will never be enough just to dabble a little here and a there.

If you wish for full satisfaction, you must give yourself completely to this work, one hundred percent. This does not mean that you have to quit your day job and go live on the street while you pursue your goal. Nor does it mean you must live like a hermit and eschew the flow of life. But when you are able to work, you must dive into your pursuit with bravery, gusto, and out-and-out abandon. And above all else, you must work!

Do not hold back or quibble over details. Do not doubt your process or be afraid. Open the floodgates and let yourself disappear into your vision. Turn yourself inside out and risk complete exposure. Dig into the raw material before you as if it were raw clay, craving your touch. No matter what you do, do it as fully and completely as you can. And like so much butterfat, the work which has the highest concentration of "you" will rise to the surface first, crying out to be tasted.

No one has ever celebrated a genius who only took things half way. Indeed, the world looks to them not just for vision and inspiration, but to take comfort in the pure dare of celebrating life as fully as possible.

This is the province of true creative genius, a place of no boundaries, no restraints, and no taboos.

✎ *Try this...*

Visit the local bookstore or library and find some books about geniuses in your field who inspire you. As you read them, keep a notebook handy for recording observations that can inform your path. Photocopy images of your heroes and hang them in your workplace. Or pick some pertinent quotations, and create a screen saver for your computer with them by using customizable screen saver software. Subscribe to any magazine that publishes success stories and trade information on people who've achieved dreams similar to yours. Keep a file of these news items clipped for easy reference.

When Talent Does and Doesn't Matter

ANOTHER PREVAILING BELIEF about talent in our world is that you either got it, or you don't. And if you don't, you might as well shell peas in the corner of a grocery for the rest of your life.

Well I, for one, say "phooey."

It may be that some of us lucked out in the gene pool more than others. Talent is a real and undeniable aspect of the success of many great achievers. There is a reason Yo-Yo Ma was at Julliard by the time he was nine. It's no mistake that Bill Gates quit Harvard to invent DOS programming. But let's talk about all the successful people out there who *don't* have extraordinary talent, for in some ways their rise is even more spectacular.

Take Madonna, for instance. Now Madonna has a fine voice, and she can certainly dance, but one could argue that her superstar status really has to do with more than just her talent. For one thing, the woman has been a human dynamo throughout her career. She has no fear whatsoever about asking for what she wants. Furthermore, she is unafraid to reinvent herself continually to stay fresh and fascinating to her fans. Madonna's genius is in her awareness of what people want, and her ability to provide it.

In other words, if you haven't got it, invent it.

We can be fairly sure Madonna never stood around twisting her hair and saying, "If only I could sing like Aretha Franklin."

Actually, Madonna didn't even set out to be a singer. She came to New York to be a dancer, drifted into drumming, and was discovered by two French promoters at Danceteria, a disco that was the epicenter of the New York club scene in the early 80's. "You should sing," they said, and so she did. Several voice lessons later, she got her first major record deal. And as the A&R person who signed her said, she just had that certain something, that superstar quality. Yet, that quality wasn't in her voice, or her packaging; it was in her presence. Madonna could sit in a chair and project the essence of a star, which I attribute to two things, crystal clear vision and a will of steel.

You don't have to have talent to be a star, but you absolutely must believe you will be one, come hell or high water. And so, you must also have an indomitable will. Your road will not be easy. You will certainly endure rejection upon rejection. You will be hated by some, and used by others if you let them. You will have to work harder than you ever thought imaginable. You might even go the route Madonna did in her early days, sleeping in abandoned buildings and eating from garbage cans. Or you could choose the safe route and get a 9-to-5 job, but here your will must be even stronger, to save you from that cozy, sleepy stupor of security that can undermine creative resolve. At any rate it won't be easy, and God knows it won't be fair.

Yet, whoever said life was fair to begin with?

Think of all the incredibly talented people out there right now who don't even have enough faith in their abilities to pick up a paintbrush or face a blank spreadsheet. I'd wager there are far more of them than the tiny minority of the less talented whose wonderful audacity keeps pushing them forward. I would also wager there is room in this world for both, so ultimately talent is not even an issue.

However...since this is an imperfect world, talent occasionally is an issue. Say you want to be a singer. If you really don't have a perfect "instrument," as the voice teachers call it, you will face frustration and it will be commensurate with the size of your dream. If you want to be Madonna, you at least have to be able to carry a tune, feel the beat, and sound pretty musical. And you have to be willing to work your tail off to make your voice and your entire persona into something salable. You have to be willing to do whatever it takes to make your dream happen. And ultimately, and perhaps most importantly, you have to be willing to fail.

You have to love yourself so much that even after years of vocal coaching, dance lessons, headshots, costume fittings, demo tapes, videos, practice gigs, social media campaigns, cold calls, business letters, auditions, rejections, constant practicing, and the endless grind of just trying to find an audience, you can walk away. And you can go quietly, knowing you did what you had to do.

If it doesn't work out, you'll have to be able to make your peace with your inability to become the next Madonna. And perhaps, in doing so, see that following your dream really wasn't all about the satisfaction of your ego, and whether or not you went on worldwide tours attracting millions of fans. What it was really about was the nourishment of your spirit. You gave yourself a profound gift, and that you didn't "succeed" was not even entirely true, for you may have even discovered that great universal secret: *the doing of the work is where true pleasure lies.*

In my own life, I learned this in 2008 when I took a one-woman show on tour called Dr. Serenity Hawkfire's Beyond Being Workshop. It was a parody of a new age workshop I performed in Fringe Festivals in Washington, D.C., Orlando and Vancouver. And it was a great gift I gave myself – the year I dedicated myself to performing. I was determined to find out if my fading dream of being a professional singer and actress was truly viable...so I used the easy access of the Fringe Festival circuit to find out.

Results were mixed. Ben Bradlee of the Washington Post gave me a positive review and I managed to win Best Comedy in D.C.. But in Vancouver, I was roundly despised; one reviewer called my show one of the 'worst performances I have ever seen', comparing me to William Hung from American Idol. Another outraged audience member stalked across my stage in the middle of my monologue and announced angrily, "I am going to bring this show down!"

You can't say they weren't listening. But after Vancouver – and two performances in which literally nobody showed – I hung up my wig and let go of that dream. And you know what? I was good with it.

I realized I didn't really want to be a great star of stage and screen after all. Yeah, I liked singing. And the acting was amusing. And it was fun to create my own show. But that's all it was for me...just fun. I had other gigs, like this, that were ultimately more meaningful to me. But best of all, I'd answered the big looming question for myself – shouldn't I be a performer? Turns out, no. And not just because I got some seriously bad reviews.

I realized that over time the wear and tear of touring a show was more than I wanted in my life. I liked my bed, thank you very much, not the ones at Motel 6. And I missed the intellectual stimulation of writing books. And best of all, I could still play my guitar and write a few songs and do a coffee house once in a while…and still be an author.

And so this particular mission got resolved, and 2008 turned out to be a very important year in my life.

If you're like me, you will have grown in subtle and important ways at the end of your dream. And so you will hopefully scan the horizon for the next dream you can appropriate, and the next adventure you can set off on. In this way, you can never lose; you can only grow, through perseverance, sweat, and the happy broadcast of your own fantastic dreams.

✎ *Try this…*

Test your will by checking off those things that apply to you:

- ❑ *There are things I want to do in life, and I'll get to them. In my nineties.*

- ❑ *If given a choice between putting in some time on my business idea, and rotating my tires, I'll go with the tires every time.*

- ❑ *I'd probably write the great American novel if I didn't have a television.*

- ❑ *I can no longer open the guest room closet because it's full of all the craft projects I started but never finished.*

- ❑ *I'd like to do something creative, but I haven't got a creative bone in my body.*

- ❑ *I definitely had more will when I was younger.*

- ❑ *I'm could do a better job than any of the so-called superstars in my field. I just don't feel like it.*

If you checked any of the above, chances are you need to re-examine where you stand with your will. Take a minute, and complete the following lists. Feel free to be brutally honest.

- ❑ *What I'm Afraid of Finding Out About My Dream*

- ❑ *What It Will Mean If I Succeed At My Dream*

- ❑ *What Will Change If I Succeed At My Dream*

- ❑ *People Who Support My Dream*

- ❑ *People Who Do Not Support My Dream*

- ❑ *What I Will Gain By Pursuing My Dream*

Read This In Case Of Emergency

UNLIKE THE REST OF LIFE, an emergency in your creative process is inevitable. When you set off on the long road to realizing your vision, you can expect some major traffic jams ahead.

This does not mean you have to get off the road altogether.

It simply means that great things are seldom created without some slowdowns, and even breakdowns, along the way.

Why is this, you might ask. I contend it is because we are only human beings and pretty limited ones at that. We're insatiable when it comes to praise, accomplishment, and looking good. And we're pretty damn pitiful when it comes to hanging with something for the long haul, and having a little faith. Bottom line: we enter most creative enterprises from the mindset of "I'll try it, but my results better be brilliant NOW...or else."

This is sort of like trying to master origami in an afternoon; it's simply not going to happen, no matter how hard we try. And not only that, by rushing the process we never get to experience the thrill of gradual mastery.

Something almost chemical happens when you try, try and try, only to master something after long and committed effort. The voices of doubt are thrown into happy submission, and for at least ten minutes you can actually be a hero in your own mind. Enough of these small triumphs and you might even accumulate some serious self-esteem. It's a slow win but it's a real one, the rewards of which are yours forever.

In the meanwhile, you will inevitably bog down. It may be that your project gets off to a fantastic start. You're clear-headed, inspired, full of ideas, and tear home from work each night, eager to get to it. That's the first week, or the first month even. Then you have a bad day. The boss calls you names. Your computer crashes. The promised promotion goes to someone else. You limp home, licking your wounds, and instead of turning to your project for a bit of soul healing, you crack open a beer and turn on the news. "I've had a helluva day," you justify. "Don't I deserve a night off?"

What you forget at such a moment is the power your work has to restore your wounded spirit. "Give me a break," you sigh. Well, okay – we all *do* deserve a night off once in a while.

But the disaster happens the next night, when you consider how easy it was to slough off your project the night before. "Still recovering," you murmur to yourself, as you head off to Happy Hour. Many months later, there's a quarter-inch of dust on the work that was originally intended to save your life. Years later, you have only a dim memory of that book you were going to write, and it's soaked in resignation and regret.

When we feel like quitting, we confuse concentrated effort with back breaking labor. The view from the downy, soft contours of our overstuffed armchairs is definitely stilted. Indeed, it seems virtually impossible to get up and make phone calls, financial projections, test recipes, or do anything. *I can't, I just can't. I'm too tired. I'm too weak. I can't even think straight. I JUST WORKED ALL DAY! How can I possibly sit down and work more???*

At that moment, it seems the effort is just plain more than we can bear.

There are always going to be moments in your process when you think yourself straight to hell. You'll convince yourself that you're too tired, too uninspired, or too depressed to carry on. A million other temptations will beckon. The mere idea of sitting at your desk will seem impossible until you actually sit down and do it. Thinking about it is what will immobilize you – just thinking about it. The actual work, if you can get yourself to begin, will probably be relatively easy.

Alex Forbes, a friend of mine who is a professional singer/songwriter calls this The Wall. In the course of nearly every song she writes, she hits a place where she just can't go on. Any spark of inspiration in what she'd already written has somehow died, and finishing the song now seems impossible. And yet, she knows she cannot just walk away and not return. So Alex sits there, noodling around, waiting for something to happen, trying not to despair.

The Wall is the place all of us hit sooner or later, yet it can also be the place of the greatest rewards. For what Alex has found is that if she can just hang in there, and press through her resistance, what lies on the other side is usually a breakthrough. An incredible bridge section that lifts the song to a whole new place, or a lyric that really gets at the heart of the matter. Every so often, however, The Wall wins. When this happens, Alex is forced to confront the fact that the song she's trying to write is really just a piece of useless fluff that doesn't deserve song status. In these cases, what The Wall demands is some serious soul-searching and truth telling. So she has come to realize that not every creative impulse needs to be pursued to completion. Alex now sees The Wall as a productive and important part of her own process.

Yet, here you are, still sitting in your comfy armchair. And the work is still sitting on your desk, staring you in the face. So, it becomes simply a matter of picking yourself out of the armchair, *even when you don't feel like doing it*, and getting to it. For it's been proven again and again: all you have to do is do it. Soon enough, the creative process will draw you in once again, warming you, enriching you, soothing all your dark defenses, welcoming you back home.

It's simply a matter of staying on the truest course.

✎ *Try this...*

The next time you need to work on your project but you "just don't feel like it", give yourself the gift of a few minutes to consider why.

Perhaps these questions will help. Answer honestly – they're for you.

1. What would you rather be doing right now?
2. If you were doing that other thing, how much would your life actually improve?
3. What's the bottom line truth about why you are avoiding your project?
4. What are you afraid of?
5. How will you feel if you don't go back to work?
6. How will you feel if you do?

How False Modesty
Kills Dreams

ONCE I SAW A STREET performer on "The Today Show", a boy not more than twelve years old skillfully juggling balls in front of an impromptu street audience. The host could help but ask, "Aren't you nervous juggling on national TV?"

The boy's eyes never strayed from his efforts – five balls that he was now juggling behind his head. "Nope," he said simply. "This is my home. This is where I belong."

Amen.

We should all be so supremely confident that we can say the unthinkable before an audience of 3.5 million. And this was the unthinkable. This kid did not have some mega-watt agent wrangling him a spot on national TV. Chances are he didn't have a PR person or even a manager. The network's crew just happened to bump into him on a sidewalk in New York, but, then, this young man already knew national TV was his home. And more importantly, he put that information into his speaking.

There has been much said about the power of our speech. In her excellent book, *Jesus CEO,* Laurie Beth Jones notes that Jesus never denigrated himself in language. Rather, in Isaiah 55:11, he said, "I declare a thing and it is done for me. My word accomplishes that which I send it out to do." This is not conceit but a simple statement of fact. Our words are our messengers. And it wasn't just Jesus who could make this happen. So it is with all our words – we really are what we speak. *Really.*

In leading my workshops, I have often heard people present work to the group by beginning with a preamble: "This probably stinks, but..." "I know this isn't any good, but..." "I tried, but this was the best I could do...." This is a weird human reflex I like to think of as The Parade of False Modesty. It's that automatic urge to publicly denigrate anything you've created – whether you secretly think it's good or not – in order to save face should the thing bomb. And it's a form of protection, so you can put your sacred work down before anyone else can. Whenever the Parade of False Modesty begins, I find myself taking a major step back in interest.

Because honestly, if you seriously thought it was so bad, you wouldn't expose us to it, would you? Those in the great Parade of False Modestly are actively willing me not to like their work, no matter how wonderful it is.

And so the Parade of False Modesty immediately snatches a little joy from its intended audience, just so that person can avoid the squirming vulnerability that comes with true self-expression. Just so he or she can squeeze into the paradigm of cool for a moment, because these days self-confidence is not totally hip. Self-confidence is a self-loving way to be, which in our ironic age doesn't' always fly.

You will never achieve what you set out to do unless you can get squarely behind it, believe in its power, and actively speak that belief. You will never make anything happen if you have to keep hiding behind false modesty. Instead you must see the work as sacred. And so remember that while this work comes from you, it is not yours alone to kick, punch, and mutilate at will. In fact, your work belongs to the rest of us, as well.

This is why you have to watch your speaking, for if you constantly insist that your work or your life is inadequate, the world will respond accordingly. Rather than seeing you as the witty, urbane individual you hope to be, we will hear your denigrating words and take that deadly step backwards. We will feel robbed, and rightly so, of the chance to see your work for itself...and you, as well. And since we will smell a self-made loser, rather than pay serious attention, we will simply pass you by.

The same is also true of the reverse. People who have the self-respect to speak kindly of themselves and their work are usually rewarded with success. Walt Whitman not only self-published the initial editions of *Leaves of Grass*, he also wrote his own glowing reviews, describing himself as "large and lusty, a naive, masculine, affectionate, contemplative, sensual, imperious person." Not unlike our juggling friend on The Today Show, Whitman knew he belonged in the public eye and had no problem saying so. And like Jesus, rather than bragging, he simply stated a fact. In doing so, he introduced himself to us as a person whose gifts we all might share. And whom we might get to know much better.

When you step forth and express yourself, the audience hears one thing: how generous a gift you are willing to give.

Think for a moment about your own speaking. Are you more in the "Oh-it's-really-nothing, just-a-little-something-I-scratched-out, it's-probably-terrible" camp, or are you more like our juggling boy on TV? When someone compliments your work, do you immediately jump down her throat with a list of its imperfections? Or do you say thank you, and allow the appreciation to sink in for a moment. Or even just know it to be true and so feel a contented peace. Giving others the chance to appreciate you is, in fact, another way to give back to them. It completes the cycle that all this giving generated in the first place, which is what your loving audience demands.

Can you imagine, for instance, if a Broadway star refused to take applause at the end of the show, but disappeared backstage too hastily instead. Wouldn't you feel cheated?

So what this all boils down to ultimately is your sense of generosity. Can you actually bring yourself to clothe your dreams in the respect and love they deserve? Can you speak of them as the powerful, wonderful creations that they are – for they are your children in a sense. Or do you have to defeat them with your words, so that they, like you, stay small and limited.

Will you give the gift or not? While the answer may ultimately lie in your actions, it truly does begin in your words.

Take a look and see. Are your words delivering the message that you want?

If You're Looking for Something to Do…

Unplug the phone, kick out kids, spouses and neighbors, and give yourself some peace and quiet. Then get a large pad of paper, several pencils or pens, and a very comfortable chair. Pour a little tea, if you like, and put on some gentle, soothing music. Then make a grand, master list of all the beliefs that keep you from moving forward with your project.

Here are some limiting beliefs that have come up in my workshops: "I'm not qualified", "I have to do this everyday or not at all!", "I'll offend too many people", "My mother will never forgive me." Press through the voice in your head that's trying to distract you, and be relentless with yourself. *Keep going until you have at least twenty-five limiting beliefs.*

Proof That Rejection Won't
Kill You

THE FIRST TIME I WROTE a novel, I heard a monotonous hum in the background the entire time. It was my mind chanting, "The first time this gets rejected I will die. The first time this gets rejected I will die."

Somehow, I managed to finish the thing, and put it into the hands of a few people I knew in the publishing business. The first rejection rolled in from the sister of a friend, a six month publishing novice who was a secretary to a famous editor. "Well, first of all," she began, "the whole thing needs a major haircut."

A haircut! A HAIRCUT!! sputtered my indignant mind. *Why don't we just shave it all off and go bald?* "Hnnh," I said, trying to be as noncommittal as I could.

"Yes, and some of these characters, Suzanne…" her voice trailed off in dismay. "How shall I put this? They were just…well…trite."

TRITE…TRITE???!!! Now my mind was under siege and

there was emergency help running in from all directions. Somehow, and I don't remember how, I managed to wind up the conversation and get off the phone before she finished her critique, whereupon I broke down into racking, heaving sobs. My book had been soundly rejected; hated, even.

Yet I did not die.

Ultimately, I signed with a literary agent who did his best to sell the book, but no one wanted to buy it. Every couple of weeks or so for an entire year, another elegant, cream-colored rejection letter with my name neatly typed on it would slip through the mail slot. For a while, they just accumulated on my desk, but then one day I shored up my soul, sat down and read them all, one by one. Immediately, I began to understand something about rejection: *it's nothing personal.*

Seriously.

In fact, almost every one of the twenty-seven rejection letters I got had a different reason for not buying my book. Some editors wanted the book, but couldn't convince their bosses or their marketing teams to buy it. Others loved the writing, but not the plot. Some didn't like the characters, or the fact that the book didn't have a stronger social relevance. But not one of them said a word about me, personally. No letter said "How can you send me a book by such a loser?" or "What kind of idiot wrote this thing?," all of which seemed entirely possible to my warped thinking. Although part of me believed – however illogically – that a personal rejection of me, Suzanne, was entirely possible.

The bottom line was that this manuscript was rejected by every single publisher in New York and never became a book…but not only did I survive, I managed to keep on writing. And publish my next novel with Random House. Because, in fact, the whole thing was a massive learning experience.

What I learned from this experience was non-attachment.

This is quite literally the difference between those who achieve their dream and those who don't

For every person who cannot put their dream in place, there is a whole lot of silent screaming going on: *Help! I might finish it. Help! It might succeed. Help! I might finally be someone and have to answer for myself in the world. HELP! Recognition will probably destroy me.* We become attached as hell to these projects. We treat them like our newborn babies and they are every bit as personal, real and important as our own flesh and blood.

The sad thing is, whether this thing flies or not isn't actually about us. It isn't us the world is waiting to embrace or ignore; it is only our work. And it's as much about the marketplace, the environment, the timing, and what you are ready to allow in your life as much as anything else. This is where non-attachment comes in.

First and foremost, *we are not our work.* We are living, breathing people who create businesses, art, ideas, and babies. But these are not, and never will be, the stuff we're made of. Still, somehow, in the process of caring a hell of a lot about something, and pouring all your sweat and blood into it, you can get terribly confused.

When a performer goes out on a stage, he may feel the audience is judging every aspect of him and his life. In fact, all that poor audience is doing is waiting to be entertained a little. They aren't commenting on the actor's looks, politics, hairstyle, or intelligence. These things are really the furthest thing from their minds. When they applaud, they are just telling a performer that they liked what she did at that particular moment, in that particular place. That's all. The rest, quite honestly, they don't even care about, nor should they be expected to.

So it isn't up to me what the world thinks of me; the world will think what it thinks and I have no control over this. Indeed, my job is simply to do the work and send it out there. That's it. End of story. It isn't up to me to make the world like me (as if I could), any more than it is up to me to determine the fate of my creative undertakings. I contend that the more honest, provocative and truly vulnerable I am with my work, the more vocal will be those who despise it. However, by the same token, my honesty will genuinely touch more people, as well.

What we have to keep remembering is to release these gifts as easily and as effortlessly as they were given to us in the first place. Not because they will make us rich, nor because they bear any significance at all. We must release these gifts simply because they flowed through us, and must now be given away – whether to the public at large, or even just to someone we love. And should we decide to go public with the work, and it gets rejected once, or even hundreds of times, we simply need to follow our instincts and keep on releasing it until we sense it is time to stop. Perhaps our work will be appreciated; perhaps it won't. And really…it doesn't even matter. That we created it in the first place means we have grown in the process – which is crucial to do in our life.

Remember the fate of Vincent Van Gogh who descended into madness as he was discovering the deepest levels of his artistic gift. Not only did he never sell a single one of his paintings – he was told by both of his psychiatrists to stop painting in order to save his own mental health. In fact, almost all of his greatest works, including his famous painting, Starry Night, were painted as he was going mad in mental institutions. Critics agree Van Gogh was at the height of his creative power in this period, and he painted furiously, against all odds. Despite the fact that by the end of his life he was suffering full convulsive seizures and the worst sort of madness. Despite the fact that doctors felt such a hectic creative pace would kill him. It ended only when Van Gogh finally walked into one of his beloved fields in southern France and shot himself, dying only a day or so later.

Each project we undertake is merely another milestone on our own particular path, a signpost which much be passed in order to reach the next one. We all have our share of scathing reviews, bitter rejections, and out-and-out failure, but ultimately, who even cares? The bigger question is, can you go to bed comforted by the thought that you came a little closer towards accomplishing your vision? Can you say to yourself, I did my work– my real work – today?

Creativity is a selfless act, demanding you give of yourself simply for the sheer love of giving. We cannot give our work to the world expecting anything in return. That this simple act requires courage is merely creativity's gift back to us.

🖎 *Try this…*

Take a moment and assess: how exactly do you handle rejection? Are you a quitter? A pouter? A take it on the chin type? Are you someone who seeks revenge? Or do you avoid rejection altogether by never starting anything in the first place?

If you're not sure, try writing down at least three times you suffered rejections. (They can be work-related, or personal.) Then carefully reconstruct exactly how you handled each experience. What is the status of those efforts today? Was anything learned?

When To Run, Not Walk,
From Helpful Advice

THERE ARE PEOPLE OUT there who would like to see you realize your dreams, and there are people who would not. These so-called friends come in all guises – family, co-workers, even teachers. For whatever reason, they relish defeat, and take comfort in helping plant the seed of yours, as well.

Avoid them at all costs.

Once you have begun the pursuit of your vision in earnest, you will be tempted to share it with the world. This may be news of your very first sale as a realtor, or perhaps some early bottles of wine from your own small vineyard, or it may be the completion of your first novel. You lug all 2500 pages of your tender new manuscript into your office, drop it at the feet of that guy across the hall who kept saying you never could do it, and stand back to enjoy a moment of smug satisfaction.

"There," you say with a smile. "Want to read it?"

The guy in the cubicle across the aisle is the wrong person to show your precious work to at this moment, for he is not, and never will be, your ally. And no matter how victorious you may feel at the huge progress you've made, your creative self is still painfully fragile. All this so-called friend has to do is shove it with his toe, and say "Yeah, sure...when I've got some time," and suddenly, your dream deflates a tiny bit.

And then, God forbid he does get some time. He'll return the manuscript, saying only, "Pretty good...I mean, I didn't believe a word of it and I thought the plot was hard to follow, but hey...what do I know?" Chances are the manuscript will find its way to a dark corner under your desk, where it will sit collecting dust far into the future.

It is my belief that the only people truly qualified to give opinions of your work are professionals – the investors, dealers, agents, critics, publishers, managers, directors, producers, admissions boards, licensing bureaus and chiefs of trade; in other words, people who get paid for their opinions. Everyone else will have an opinion, of course, but that by no means implies that you should listen to it. Or even expose yourself to it.

And above all, take special care with your family. If you come from one in which competition has a part in the dynamic, do not do this. You will be hurt.

Still, we are gluttons for punishment. In some sick way we *want* the guy across the hall to hate it, so then that ever-chiming voice of doubt can be right for once. Then we're off the hook! No one else has to ever see the work! All the hard work, risk, and discomfort is over! Blissfully, we can sink back into our armchair and assume permanent couch potato position, and just forget the whole damn dream business that started all this in the first place. So we're defeated, we smirk, reaching for a fistful of chips. Who gives a damn? At least we can relax for a change.

And when it comes to our family, how we want Mom or

Dad or our sisters and brothers to love and acknowledge what we have done. Which is not only possible but desirable and good for some of us. And for others of us – we know who we are – that's just not going to happen. Again, use caution here.

Our sister or the guy across the aisle hates our book, and so we've just died a thousand small deaths. And yet, the phoenix can and will rise from the ashes, as we proceed to do what we should have done in the first place. We go to the library and research agents, managers, licensing bureaus or whoever the gatekeeper is for our chosen field. We locate books and professional organizations where we can find information on how best to approach these folks, learning whatever etiquette may be required.

We get the small education we need to make our mark, and join clubs or enroll in classes that help us learn how to market our efforts. We network, calling everyone we ever knew, asking if they happen to know anyone who might be helpful. And then and only then, after giving ourselves the support we need to proceed with care, we pass our creation on to maybe one or two trusted, true friends. *These are friends who honestly want to see us succeed.* (You know who these people are, and if you don't, ask the Universe to send a few your way. Everyone needs at least one ally.)

Our supporters will have ideas for us, and many of them may be of value. If they happen to be proficient in our chosen field, then all the better. But remember one thing: they are not, and never should become our gods. Treat their opinions as nothing more than what they are – opinions.

My father, John Falter, was an artist who as a very young child exhibited a natural talent for draftsmanship. When he was fifteen, his parents took him to the nearest big city, and showed samples of cartoons he'd been publishing in the local paper to a successful, syndicated cartoonist there. "This boy will never be a great cartoonist," the man decreed. "He draws too well." My father so revered this man's opinion he basically wrote off cartoon work for the rest of his life.

Even though he became one of the most important illustrators of his generation, a small part of him always longed to do cartoons. A number of times over the years, he submitted cover ideas to The New Yorker, each with legitimately funny concepts, but they were always turned down. And he was forever making little funny pencil sketches of things he saw happening all around him. Perhaps the cartoonist was right, but maybe he wasn't. What's certain is that my father never felt he could be a cartoonist after this pronouncement. And I believe part of him wished he could have been...despite his success as an illustrator. He never published a cartoon again.

The opinions of mentors and teachers need to be treated with a degree of caution, as well. Far too often they teach not to inspire and encourage their students into working, but to snag a precious audience and feed their ravenous egos. Beware of teachers who make denigration part of their teaching – constructive criticism should never be confused with public humiliation. In fact, criticism can never even be heard by a student, unless it is delivered in a gentle, soul-informing way: a way that acknowledges the student's own innate gifts.

Also, beware of classes where the teacher sits back and turns the students into teachers. These free-for-alls can turn into slash and burn sessions that are more about competition than anything else. I remember an advertising copywriting class I took once, taught by an award winning creative director, in which the students (90% of whom had never worked in advertising) were challenged to "find the holes" in each other's work. By mid-semester, fifty percent of the class had stopped coming. By the end, only three of us remained. It is safe to say a whole lot of learning did not go on there.

True self-expression demands incredible vulnerability, and so we must treat our work as the precious gift that it is. The urge to share may be wonderful and irrepressible, but we need to be smart about it. For this is not ours, this thing we have created; it's divine work that has been put in our hands, however briefly. To be careful stewards, we must proceed with open eyes, fully cognizant of the minefield ahead. Only then will our work find the souls it was intended to touch, and only then will our job be complete.

🖎 *Try this...*

Make two lists:

* People Who Support My Project
* People Who Do Not Support My Project

When making these lists, get in touch with how they've made you feel in the past. Do you get any red flags or unpleasant memories? Do you recall times when you felt very safely held and understood? Use these are your guidelines.

Notice if some people you thought were your supporters make their way on to the opposing list as well. If so, they should be considered People Who Do Not Support My Project. Be honest here, and these lists will be useful tools for getting the support you need. For here is a clear list of people you can safely share your work with. And a list of those you can't share with at this time.

Then, try this....

Begin a file filled with encouraging notes, e-mails and letters you collect along your path. These could be messages from supporters, parents, kids, colleagues and professionals – anyone who was genuinely touched by what you're doing, and wants to support your efforts. The file can even include rejection letters from people who see and state the value of your work. Feel free to plunge in and read them whenever your morale needs a boost.

In Praise of Failure

ONE REASON MANY PEOPLE never get around to pursuing their dream is what psychologists and other analytical types call "fear of failure." Essentially, one is so paralyzed by the mere possibility that they might fail, that they do back flips to avoid such a catastrophe. Well, to any of you who might be feeling this way, I have only a few choice words: get over yourself.

Not only is failure an essential and important part of your progress, it is unavoidable. No matter what you set out to do, sooner or later there will be a failure, whether it is a complete and total belly flop at the onset that redirects your course, or a later one, after you've become an established success. Basically, experiencing failure is like arguing with your spouse; nobody wins. Furthermore, nobody wants to do it, but sooner or later it's bound to happen.

Handled intelligently, failure won't be a disaster at all. Rather, it will yield all sorts of important information about your well-being and your conduct in life.

While it may seem a gross generalization to say that nobody can avoid failure, it's true. More often than not, failure is simply the smashing of our expectations. It is the rerouting of our vision onto a different course. And while we hardly like the experience, it is wonderful in a way, because it shakes us from our smugness. It reminds us how little we actually know about this path that we're on. It pulls us back up to the job of reinventing ourselves, returning us to the essential work of creation. If our egoes will just let us get on with it, failure calls us forward once again, as creators.

There is a wonderful story about Stephen Crane. His novel, *Maggie: A Girl of the Streets* was found to be too realistic and grim for commercial publishing of the 1890's. So, unable to find a publisher, the author published it himself, only to sell 100 copies. Unfortunately, Crane had spent his entire savings on the book so he was forced to burn the remainders for fuel. However, one of the few copies that was left reached William Dean Howells, who then helped Crane get another manuscript published, *The Red Badge of Courage*. After its phenomenal success, *Maggie* was republished to roaring success.

Then there's Cyrus H. McCormick. McCormick, a farmer's son, dedicated his entire adult life to the development of a horse-drawn reaping machine, a project his father had begun. After several years of refinement, he finally got the design right. Then he spent nine years trying to convince farmers, who had been harvesting their fields by hand with scythes, that his invention actually worked. There were no buyers. The panic of 1837 followed and McCormick went bankrupt; the bank repossessed everything except his reaper, which they decided wasn't worth a dime. Which was fortunate, since McCormick was not about to give up.

After two more years of doggedly dragging farmers out into fields and demonstrating his machine, he finally sold one.

Four years later, he'd sold 50 of them. McCormick tried everything to market his invention – money-back guarantees, payment plans, and testimonial advertising, which was unheard of then. Six years later, he'd sold 3,000 reapers. Then he demonstrated the machine in Europe, and before a skeptical crowd, harvested 74 yards of wheat in 70 seconds. After a moment of stunned silence, the crowd began to cheer wildly. McCormick took home international medals and the applause of the press. By the time of his death, 33 years later, McCormick's reaping machine had amassed a fortune of 10 million dollars, and launched a company known today as International Harvester.

Michelangelo at San Lorenzo has a similar story. Michelangelo (who was regularly beaten by his father for wanting to be an artist) began the church at San Lorenzo after establishing himself as Italy's preeminent monumental sculptor. The artist was originally hired to design and sculpt all the statuary on the church facade. Another architect had been hired to design the church itself. After two months of working with the architect, however, Michelangelo decided only he, himself, could design a building magnificent enough to house his sculpture. Yet, at this point in his life, Michelangelo had never designed any architecture. Michelangelo won the commission and, thinking big as usual, declared that he would "domesticate the mountains" and create "the mirror of architecture and sculpture of all Italy."

That's what I'm talking about.

Michelangelo set out to create a facade for San Lorenzo that included twenty enormous columns, each made from a massive piece of marble. Each piece would have to be hauled by horse-drawn sledge, cart, boat, and finally on foot, from the other end of Italy. Four years later, Michelangelo had opened a new quarry, built roads to it, designed a massive crane for hauling the marble, devised a pinion system for moving the loads around steep, twisting mountaintop roads, and employed an entire army of 300 quarry men and stone movers.

Michelangelo personally spent more than eight months just checking out veins of marble. He was nearly killed when one of the columns, because of a faulty iron ring, smashed to the ground as it was being lifted out of the quarry. And this was only one of seven columns he quarried – five more disappeared en route. Only one column actually made it to San Lorenzo, where it still lies today, covered with moss in a ditch near the church.

Later that year, the Pope who commissioned the work died, Michelangelo's contract was terminated, and the project was given to other designers to complete more simply. Michelangelo wrote to the Vatican: "I am not charging to this account the fact that I have been ruined over the said work at San Lorenzo; I am not charging to this account the enormous insult of having been brought here to execute the said work, and then having it taken away from me…I am left with two handfuls of toil and a striving after wind."

When he wrote this, Michelangelo did not know he was going on to spend the last third of his career as one of the world's great architects. Nor that the facade of San Lorenzo would always remain unfinished, and his abandoned column left exactly where he placed it, out of respect for what he had begun. All he knew was that he'd tried architecture and failed miserably. Yet, the architectural triumph of the Medici Chapel still awaited him, as did St. Peter's. At this moment, Michelangelo's sense of failure was the same as anyone's. It seemed like a hopeless situation from which nothing good could ever come.

History has proven otherwise, however. The facade for San Lorenzo took Michelangelo into an entirely new era in his career. So, like all failures, it was simply a rearrangement of plans, a sudden and unexpected blow to one's expectations.

Most failure is not an end in itself, but a beginning disguised as an end. The only true failure would have been for Michelangelo to stop caring and stick his sculpture into a facade he considered unworthy. The only true failure would have been for him to arrest that part of himself that refused to acquiesce. That would have been the death of his vision, and a strike against his almost unbearable passion, an emotional force so powerful the townspeople gave it a name: Michelangelo's *terribilita* (Michelangelo's 'awfulness'.)

More recently a successful jewelry designer named Lorelei took one of my workshops. She had been laid off from her job as a sales rep for a large jewelry company. At the time she was devastated, even though a small voice in the back of her head kept reminding her that she didn't really want to sell jewelry…she wanted to design it. Yet, Lorelei had no design background or education. All she had was an intense interest in color, and jewelry, and enough savings to live on for a few years. So she began.

Lorelei's early designs were dismal things made out of wood, crystal and hardware wire, and they were inclined to fall apart. Still, she gamely started trying to sell them to her old network of department store buyers. Sales contacts politely declined. Friends would say things like, "Not bad for a first try."

A major retailer finally took pity and stocked some of her pieces, not one of which sold. Then Lorelei stumbled on to using Czech glass beads and things began to look up. She got some technical instruction, and went over to the Czech Republic where she connected with a local glass manufacturer who took a week off from work to drive her around town, looking for a source for beads. Why? Because he recognized a fellow creator and wanted to help.

Not long after that Lorelei exhibited at her first trade show, and received an order so big that her entire family and most of her friends had to sit around the dining table assembling earrings night after night.

Lorelei went out on branch after branch after branch to build her business, never looking down to notice the dizzying falls she could slip into, or stopping to weigh the many attendant risks. As she puts it, "What was important was that I stuck with my idea in the beginning and just kept giving myself time to keep trying new designs. I always knew this could work because I wanted it so much." Lorelei's business grew to include a small factory with a staff of six, producing about 15,000 pieces of jewelry per year. She considers herself extraordinarily lucky. I consider her wise, for she honestly knows the truth about failure and persistence.

There really is no such thing as failure. There is only the rearrangement of plans, and the surrender of ego. There is only the twist in the road we never expect. As long as we remain true to our vision and ourselves, we simply cannot fail. That is all we have to remember.

🖎 *Try this…*

Make a list of the five most important failures in your life, and what they led to. Were they true failures, or were they simply a rearrangement of your plans? What did you learn or gain? Did you ever make use of these 'failures'? Have you forgiven yourself yet? How can you make use of them now?

The Benefits of Wishing for Too Much

As a nation, we are constipated wishers. And who can blame us? Most of us grew up in homes where epithets like "Be careful what you wish for. You just might get it!" were constantly being hurled in our faces.

Be careful what you wish for. You just might get it. What exactly does this mean, anyway? I interpret it to mean don't bother to consciously desire happiness, challenge, and growth, because you, oh worthless one, couldn't begin to handle it.

I also interpret it to mean we are doomed to a life of fruitless wishing for fruitless pursuits that would probably be so stressful they'd end up killing us.

Well, excuse me for living.

I am a passionate believer in wishing, and think we should all do far more of it. And yet, there is a definite art to it, which I have learned from not only the occasional wish come true, but from a thousand or so wishes that have been dashed.

The magic is this: my wishes only work when I really believe I deserve them. On the other hand, if I don't believe, I usually don't receive.

An example. From time to time, in a casual, backhanded sort of way, I've wished for millions dollars. It's a Pavlovian response, an automatic answer when the subject of wishing comes up. Sure I'd love a bulging suitcase of cash; who wouldn't? But in the very next second, I also often had the thought that I'd never get it. Millions of dollars just doesn't fit in my radar screen. It's too vast a sum, too huge a gift. It doesn't seem possible, not given the little person I really, actually, secretly am. And so my wish dries up and blows away, another fruitless thought.

The truth is, I could never accept millions dollars unless I believed I'd done something spectacular enough to merit it. And hey…what have I done lately to deserve it? When I tell the truth, I don't really want the cash. What I want is work that's worth millions of dollars to the world. Then my wish feels stronger, more plausible, truly worth wishing for. It seems like something I might even deserve.

Recently I was looking through the paper and saw an ad for a one-night-only benefit performance of unpublished songs by the late Jonathan Larson, the creator of "Rent." I have been a huge "Rent" fan, and immediately thought to myself that I had to see it. Then I noticed the cost of tickets: $150. Without further ado, I turned the page, but the wish had already been made. I'd connected with my deep desire to go. I didn't question that I deserved to be there. I could even see myself walking into the theater, ready to soak up every last exhilarating ounce of it. I'd only thrown it out because of simple financial logistics, so as far as I knew, I wasn't going. Then I promptly forgot about it.

Three days later, on the afternoon of the performance, a friend called me, offering me a free ticket to see the show. We had orchestra seats that night, and I learned once again the power of deep desire. I was merely adding proof to the fact that you really do get what you want in life.

When my wishes haven't worked out, it's because they came from my stomach instead of my heart. Actually, I really have no idea what part of my body the wishes came from, but they felt like stomach wishes, because they were so incredibly gluttonous. For instance, when I published my first novel, my wishes had me lounging on Letterman's couch, languidly tossing out bon mots while millions watched and adored. My wish was for instant celebrity – validation of the very invalidated little person who dwelled within.

Now, nearly 25 years later, I realize I never could have handled instant celebrity. My infrastructure was weak and unstable; and my grasping, needy desire for this following was all about me…not them, my precious readers. I was very much a work in progress who hadn't yet opened her heart. But isn't that the way with stomach wishes?

My wishes had me lunching with Larry King, turning down screenplay offers left and right, and raking in major literary awards, not to mention escaping from my horribly crowded book signings through a back door to my waiting limo. The reality of publication included a handful of tiny write-ups in tiny newspapers, book signings where I read to three people I was related to, and a book that almost immediately went out of print.

This is what happens when wishes are all about me! me! me! and not about them! them! them! At the end of the day, the point of publishing a novel was actually not so I could have my fifteen minutes in the public glare, but so I could offer my readers something they might find moving and helpful. The point was to give these people a gift.

My wishes have since changed accordingly. I'm learning that

just wishing for success is simply not enough – mainly because it can be such a narcissistic snare. A way to finally prove to…say…my mother or my siblings or anyone else watching that hey, I'm great! I have a following! I am worth something!

Ah…the rutted road to wish fulfillment.

Now things are different. For me be truly humble and authentic with this work, and to share it from a place about deep service, my wishes have to be all about taking care of my reader. Am I sharing my heart as best I can? Am I speaking my own unspeakable truths? Am I being as clear, concise and evocative as I can be? Because that, I know, is the only way anyone will truly be moved by this work.

When I create from that place, then success and Letterman and the rest of it is the last thing on my mind. Instead, I let Spirit flow through me in this work, and neatly get out of the way as I enjoy the frisson of pure, joyful creation.

And so my wishes – when in right alignment – melt into the work itself, and I begin to have the purest kind of fun. Which is just how it all should be.

In setting out to do our work, we have to keep remembering that we're in the business of giving gifts. In order to give these gifts to those for whom they are intended, we have to get out of our head and sink into our heart. That is where the truest creating lives anyway – and where the most joy is to be found.

Wishes help this process, because they force us to focus on exactly what feels good and true. And while we ultimately have little control of outcomes, we do have our wishes and the lovely path they bring. And so we have the pure, joyful buzz of creating. When our wishes come from the heart, and not the stomach, we forget all about things like worthiness and validation. Finally we surrender to fun…and so big things can finally happen for us.

Which brings us around to the title of this chapter. Say you spent your vacation shooting color pictures of turtles in the Galapagos, and they're really great. They are by far the best pictures you've ever shot, even though you've been nursing your amateur photography habit for years. Everyone who sees them is struck by their power, and all around you the feedback is positive. So what do you do with them?

Your secret wish is that some magazine like National Geographic will buy them, but of course you know this is completely unrealistic. (*"Not a chance in hell! Forget about it! I shot these on your vacation, for God's sake!"*) On the other hand, your brother-in-law the dentist said he'd hang one in his waiting room. So you figure that's about as good as it's going to get, there's no point in submitting them anywhere, and you plod off to your brother-in-law's, negatives in hand. Right?

Wrong, wrong, wrong.

Instead of leaping to the chintziest of possible conclusions, try sitting there for a while and thinking about where this work really needs to go. Forget about your ego for once, and feeding the gluttonous maw of your self-defeat. Instead, try to connect with the hopeful wishes that are still in there, desperately trying to make contact. And while you're at it, try to cut through any overinflated stomach wishes that may have you feeling a bit bloated. If you can, let yourself really, truly wish for something as deeply as you ever have. Make it something that is of real importance to you.

It's a frightening prospect, getting what you want. Even more frightening is letting yourself believe that you deserve it. Yet, this is what separates the people who achieve their dreams from the rest of us. Their passion is so strong for their vision, that they are naturally audacious about it. It never occurs to them to wonder whether they're good enough to sell their pictures to National Geographic. These people just naturally think big, so they're more concerned with getting the right pictures in the right places. For them, deserving success isn't even a conversation. They're just going with what's in their heart.

The same can be true for you, but again, only if you think you deserve it. Listen to your instincts about where your work needs to go and whom it needs to reach. Perhaps the audience for it will be small and select. On the other hand, perhaps it will sweep the nation.

Be a good parent to your work, and have high hopes for it. You deserve it, as do those the work is intended to reach.

By all means, wish for too much. The results may truly astound you.

✎ *Try this…*

Buy yourself a special blank notebook, one you really like. Personalize it by sticking a favorite image on it, or writing some key quotations or notes in a visible place on the cover or inside. Then take your notebook to a favorite place: a hammock, a coffee bar, a beach, a park, any place that resonates with your spirit. I like to make my wishes on long train rides.

Start writing down your wishes in your book – the really true ones you haven't given yourself much time to acknowledge. Let them flow however they do, in lists, words, or even as detailed scenarios. Try not to judge them or get into how you'll implement them. Instead, just let them pour out of you, one after another. Make a regular habit of connecting with your wishes, and when they materialize, make a note of that in your book, as well.

Why Power is More
Than a Trip

THERE IS ONE UGLY question that really drives this book. It's a simple question, yet for some reason it's one that no one ever wants to hear.

How big are you willing to be?

Not how big are you going to be, but how big are you *willing* to be, emphasis on the word "willing."

The power with which you waltz through this life is absolutely and completely in your own hands, and it can be tremendous. Your mind can gain infinite wisdom and prosperity, and your body can produce extraordinary health and strength. Your mind and body will do this all for you, but only if you are willing.

If you aren't willing to think and be big, what you get is what many of us have: substantial debt, bad backs, annoying children, excruciating jobs. And with that comes a passel of longing for other people's homes, lawns, jobs, lives, kids and credit ratings. In this country, especially, we believe in the power of more money to lubricate the wounds.

We see a larger house as the panacea to a stultifying marriage. We imagine a big vacation to be the thing that will finally bond our families. Yet, all of those problems are quite solvable within the confines of our too-small, inadequate homes, on the average weekend, behind the lawns crawling with crabgrass. All it requires is for us to give up being small and whiney, and finally start to get big.

The process begins with a question: what is it that you get from your current arrangement? You're definitely getting something. Inadequate jobs are excellent places to hide. Lousy marriages are wonderful protectors of the soft part of your heart. (God forbid you are actually connect in a way that means something to you – you might get hurt!) And having no money relieves one of all those nasty adult responsibilities, like paying taxes, investing in IRA's, and saving for one's future.

The mind is wonderfully literate this way, for it truly will produce whatever you want – and by this I don't mean just your surface desires, but those that dwell in that deep place far within. For here is the seat of your power, the place you visit in visualizations, prayer, repeated mantras, chants, dreams and all means that tap into your subconscious. While I do not know exactly where this big, black place is, I know when I'm in touch with it.

When I find that place, my desires run as clear and unimpeded as water in a stream. They're not weighted down with the freight of a million doubting thoughts. They're not scrambling over a mountain of mental logistics. They simply are. *I want to lead workshops. I want to write novels. I want to have a wonderful marriage. I want a son and a daughter.* They are simple moments of truth we take possession of, know in our soul, and don't let go of, no matter what. And they are forces that pull us to them, through thick and thin and past obstacle after obstacle. They are, in fact, the still, small voices that never, ever gives up on us.

So why aren't we all walking about like the studly bastions of power we actually are?

Simply because we don't think we're worth it.

We stick ourselves in so-so jobs because this is all we assume we can handle. We believe the ho-hum salary that goes along with it is all we deserve. Like anorexics, we refuse to allow ourselves more than just barely enough money, health, love, sex, or creativity to stay alive because deep down inside we are ashamed. Still we insist loudly that such meager crumbs are all that is possible. We can't get the job we love! We tried to make it living our dream – and it was a dud! We are just *stuck* with this stupid illness, this annoying marriage, this crappy place to live…this inadequate life.

Yet behind it all we know the truth: we believe we are guilty of a thousand unmentionable sins. And so we muddle on.

Why even bother trying to emerge?

In fact, we are afraid. Our power is like a huge and unnatural tool to us – a roaring chainsaw, when in a life designed for a nail file. Yet the things that chainsaw can and will do for us are amazing when applied with care and precision. And how we crave them at times. All that is required is that we wake up, open our eyes and finally start taking responsibility for our happiness.

I received perfect proof of this in an e-mail from a reader in Minnesota named Barbara. Barbara was working for a high-powered general counsel who got promoted to president of the company, which meant a quantum leap in work for his support staff. When this happened, Barbara had the distinct thought that there had to be a better way to make a living,. She scratched out some notes on starting a business that would help people organize their households. She put the notes away and for four years didn't think much more about them. Then Barbara started to burn out.

Finally Barbara quit her job, unsure of exactly what she would do next. A small miracle promptly followed. As a thank-you gift from her boss, she received a day at a spa. So, as she tells it, "there I was, eating my lunch in this lovely spa, reading Spa Magazine, and I find an article about a woman in Washington state who does exactly what I thought about doing five years earlier – organizing people. This was my epiphany, and then there was no stopping me."

Barbara tracked down the woman in the article, spent an hour on the phone with her, and set up shop. Her business, now a few years old, is going strong and she is living life as the truly powerful person she was meant to be. By having the courage to live up to her potential and walk away from the stress (and security) of an unsatisfying job, Barbara gave herself permission to be big. Her story is impressive.

We must allow ourselves to see what is in front of us, and not merely ride along on the old, popular interpretation. We have to listen to what people around us say, and concentrate on what's coming out of their mouths instead of what's about to come out of ours. We must constantly assess and evaluate from a place of deep clarity, a place that is unaffected by politics, favor, trends, or the ephemeral illusion of coolness. Use those old first grade rules for crossing the street: Stop, Look and Listen. All of these are things we were designed to do.

Our power demands we act deliberately. It has no time for sidestepping. We must be unafraid to be utterly honest, to honor our gut feelings and to say and do the unpopular when necessary. We have to give up our addiction to other people's opinions, and surrender to the freedom of acting with strength and courage. We will have detractors, just as detractors always collect around anything new and powerful. That won't change.

What does change when you start to live from your power is that you care progressively less and less about those voices of doom and all their vicious barbs.

Instead you begin to listen to yourself…and honor that beautiful wellspring of intuition, wisdom and grace.

So you start to see the humor in your own petty concerns. You may even begin to delight in people's taunting jibes, or the lacerations of the press, because along with power comes massive amounts of perspective and commitment. You will be able to see another person's snipes as a sad expression of their own weak character. And so you may know compassion. Your ability to empathize will be heightened; in this way little anyone says or does will hurt you.

Your power can carry you through whatever you undertake, just like Luke Skywalker's protective "Force." While you may not always succeed, you will remain relatively unscathed in the process. Your projects may "fail" on a public level – they may not elicit many sales, or become critical hits. But for you they will always be precious and sacred – acts of creation that you truly believed in and loved, and so they helped you grow. Behind any failure will still be your own substantial joy and pride.

Best of all, you will know you are living as you were meant to live at your maximum potential. The nagging thoughts of "I should" and "I really ought" will dry up and disappear as you move deeper and deeper into your correct alignment. The work that lies ahead will no longer seem intimidating. Instead, you will look forward to digging in with gusto. As you merrily push past your old limitations and see the ripple effect of your power at play, you will connect once again with that core happiness. And so you will know your vital place on earth.

Whether you realize it or not, you were hard wired for this power long ago. Plugging into it requires no more than simply letting go of the fear, deciding you're worth believing in, and doing that which comes naturally.

The small, still voice within will tell you exactly what to do – all you have to do is listen. Whether you know it or not, the Force is already with you.

✎ *Try this...*

Spend one week treating yourself as the truly powerful person you are. Get up an hour early each day and take the walk you've been meaning to take. While you are walking, connect with your spiritual guidance [see page XX], and create an affirmation for yourself that confirms your sense of power. (Affirmations are little statements that help us create what we want in life. When said repeatedly, they seep into your subconscious where all manifestation begins. An affirmation can be any phrase that expresses what you want to have happen – they are always positive, proactive, and set in the present tense. They also work well for calming fears you may identify as holding you back. One of my personal favorites is "It's safe to trust my power." Another one I've used for several years is, "My work moves millions of people around the world.")

At least three times during the appointed week, take yourself to a place that feeds your soul – a museum, a forest, a concert, any place that calls to you. Make a special point of taking care of yourself that week. Don't have the usual glass of wine every night, and see how much better you sleep. If you smoke or drink copious amounts of caffeine, make a decision to stop for the week. Nurture yourself with food that's good for you. For one week, cut out junk food and venture into whole grains and fresh produce, and drink water instead of soda for a change. Unplug the television and let your answering machine pick up the phone. After your life is free of the usual distractions, make a point of doing the work you were meant to do for at least five of the seven days this week.

At the end of the week, take yourself out for a sumptuous meal and assess how your feelings of power have changed.

Why You Are Here

IF THERE IS ONE final thought I could leave you with, it would have to be this: remember why you are here.

I would suggest it is probably not so you can do the hang thing in front of old Seinfeld reruns, or to compulsively keep house or cruise catalogs. You and I both know there's something bigger on the Universal agenda for you, and you have already been called upon many times to fan those smoldering embers. Otherwise, you probably wouldn't be reading this book.

Well, I'm telling you once again. Make a fire and this time, let it rage.

Your purpose in life is sacred territory; it is the beloved idea you wish you could get to if you just had the time, the project you started once but stopped when it scared you. Your purpose in life is not necessarily that useful, responsible, tax-paying thing you do every day from nine to five. It is bigger than that, for it is predicated on what pours from your soul when you bother to open it up. And it demands every ounce of courage, love, sweat, and perseverance you've got.

Your purpose in life remains in the hands of God, until you decide to live dangerously and reach for it.

There are no guarantees what the results will be, for purposes aren't always necessarily about results. Your purpose in life may actually be to start restaurants that fail . But you must start them, and go through all the marvelous crenellations of that process in order to grow in the ways you were intended to grow.

Your purpose is simply about the fulfillment of your own private destination as a person in this lifetime. Therefore, it's the quality of the ride that counts, not whether you "get there" or not. I even question whether there really is a "there," for the act of creating is, in and of itself, such a splendid, soul-enriching thing to begin with. Create what you envision, then toss it out into the world. If it catapults you to huge financial reward and screaming success, if Oprah, Dr. Phil and the rest of the world clamor for interviews, then that's basically gravy. Your project will have already provided you with the fat steak of fulfilling your vision.

Dream your dream, then dare to stake your claim on it. What you will receive will be all the riches of the world — you, as originally intended.

How to Make Time for
Your Soul

- **Unplug your television.** Even better, completely remove it.

- **Cancel your subscriptions.** Get rid of anything you don't read.

- **Make regular 'soul' time every day.** If you're a morning person, get up one hour earlier and dig into your projects. If you're a night person, stay up one hour later.

- **Say no to your boss.** Leave at 5:00 or 5:30. Chances are, you'll find you're more valuable than you thought you were. Also, you'll probably find you work with increased efficiency. Offer to come in one hour earlier, if need be, to leave time for your evening classes, projects, events.

- **Don't waste your lunch hour eating.** Bring lunch to work, eat it briefly at your desk, and then get out there and do what really matters to you.

- **Stop agreeing to do things you don't truly want to do.**

This includes volunteering, meeting friends and family, and serving on committees.

- **Redesign your work schedule.** Create one day or several afternoons a week to concentrate on the things you really want to do in life. Explore flex-time alternatives in your workplace. Consider telecommuting, working from a home office, or going free-lance with your company. If giving up corporate benefits seems impossible, get in touch with self-employed advocacy groups like Support Services Alliance, Inc., to find out about their various insurance plans for members.

- **Put the kids to bed earlier.** Establish 'grown up' time, a time zone when all children are in bed (even if they're only looking at books or listening to tapes before going to sleep) and the adults get to have a little room to breath.

- **Multi-task.** Fold nurturing practices into your routine, such as meditating or praying while you walk, or practicing an instrument while dinner cooks. Rather than stare at work on the train, take a book you've been wanting to read. Books on tape are especially good for this.

- **Rethink your routine.** Jot down your daily routine, then reevaluate it. Does reading the newspaper cover-to-cover do as much for you as working on the furniture you keep wishing you had time to refinish?

- **Cut corners cooking.** Take advantage of gourmet take-out and grocery-store fast foods, such as prewashed salad, precut vegetables, and marinated chicken.

- **Let calls go to voice mail.** Better yet, encourage friends to e-mail you, instead of calling. Or contact you on Facebook, and only check once per day

- **Consider a 'dumb phone'.** Smart phones require time and attention – for things like constantly checking email and playing Words With Friends. (Pre-paid plans on a basic phone are much cheaper, too.)

- **Create your own sanctuary.** Make a room of your own, preferably with a door. Hang a Do Not Disturb sign on it, and don't let others interrupt you. Family and friends will honor your request to have some time for yourself only if you do, too.

- **Quit volunteering so much.** Cut your list back to only those things that truly enrich you. Give other people a chance to do the rest.

- **Divide up the housework.** Hand over the laundry and vacuuming to your mate. Teach your children to do dishes, cook meals and mop floors. And be willing to give up control of the end results. Read Patricia H. Sprinkle's book, *Children Who Do Too Little ; Why Your Kids Need to Work Around the House (and How to Get Them to Do It)* for terrific pointers on how to make this happen.

- **If you can't relax your standards, delegate.** Hire local teenagers, professional housecleaners, or even a temp service to help you clear out your desk, answer correspondence, pay bills, organize closets, walk the dog – whatever you can give up that makes more time for you.

- **Do something you truly love.** Once you've created this time for yourself, use it wisely. Take on the challenges and dreams that really will improve your life. Chances are that once you start, it will be very hard to stop.

How to Start a Joy Group

FIRST OF ALL, LET'S ask the obvious question: what is a Joy Group?

A Joy Group is a free meeting that is held every few weeks or even once a month with some like-minded others who have dreams to pursue and would like to put the ideas in this book to use. It can be held live, or online. A Joy Group is your way to travel your rutted roads together, drawing inspiration from each other's successes, and finding reassurance when the going gets tough.

Okay, you say, but *why* start a Joy Group?

Because at ten o'clock at night when you're sitting alone in front of your completely bogged down screenplay and you've just gotten rejection #23 on your other screenplay, it's nice to know you're not alone and that you actually do have some supporters out there.

Because when you find yourself cleaning the fish tank instead of calling potential investors, it helps to know someone is waiting for you to make those calls.

And because when miracles finally happen and the earth moves and you achieve your dream, it's the sweetest thing in the world to share that with friends who really know what you've been through.

Along with reading this book to get the wheels turning on achieving your dreams, you may also need real, live, human support on an on-going basis. The perfect way to make that happen is with a Joy Group. By showing up regularly at Joy meetings, you will have an automatic schedule imposed on your dream. You will also be forced to be accountable for your progress.

For a large chunk of my professional life, I worked with a career coach in New York City. A career coach is sort of like a personal trainer for your soul – I saw mine twice a month for support and guidance on reaching my goals in my career and my personal life. The main reason I hired a coach, however, was because I desperately needed to become accountable for my dreams. I needed to show up somewhere every week and report what I'd done to a person who cared. Yes, my coach and I did a lot of exercises, and talking, and probing of my soul. Yet, it was mostly by his presence in my life and his willingness to listen that I moved from being a frightened wannabe writer with half-baked resolve to a published novelist who wrote faithfully every day and totally changed her life.

There is no question in my mind that we need supporters like coaches and Joy Groups, and just good friends to tackle our dreams.

When a good support system is firmly in place, the obstacles no longer seem so big or daunting. You will still feel like quitting occasionally, but now you'll have a friend to call who will be able to talk you through it. You'll have a place to show up where your excuses will not necessarily be tolerated, and your triumphs will be celebrated. You will be supported, possibly for the first time, by others who truly care whether your dream is getting any closer. Furthermore, your group will be tuned in to the truth of exactly what your vision requires, so there really can be no escaping – not if you truly want to achieve your dream.

For those of you who've used the lack of a deadline or support in your life to allow your dreams languish, starting a Joy Group may be the best thing you've ever done.

Here are a few key questions to consider in helping your group take shape:

How Do You Start a Joy Group?

First of all, locate some interested friends you trust – honest-to-God supporters who are really in your corner, and who will accept the same from you. (Before you choose them, read the chapter titled "When to Run Not Walk From Helpful Advice" and do the exercise that follows.) If you're not sure you know anyone who fits in this category, post a sign in a local bookstore, at a church or temple, or possibly on-line. Chances are that others who've read this book will already be primed on what such work requires.

If you find you don't have many friends who are up for this, consider finding more participants by starting a Joy Meetup group. Meetup.com is a wonderful website that helps live groups of all types assemble. Simply go to the website at www.meetup.com and dig in. It's free to start a local group. You can even niche it if you want, which works well in more populated areas. Think Joy Groups for Stay at Home Moms, or Retirees, or Empty Nesters, or 12 Steppers or Weight Watchers or…well, anything! Meetup helps you create a nifty little sign up page for your group. You moderate who joins and accesses the group, and you can even invite your Facebook buddies to participate. Voila…instant group!

If you don't want to meet live, you can also make your Joy Group virtual and hold it with a free teleconference bridge. (This is a great solution if you live in a less populated area, and/or wish to niche the group online to a specific interest.) On Free Conference call, at www.freeconferencecall.com, you can host up to 96 participants for free. You simply provide participants with a call in number and a pin code to join you. Callers will only pay their usual charges that appear on their phone bill.

Consider using your own social media community, such as Facebook, Pinterest, or Linked In to fill your virtual Joy group. Simply create a Facebook page for your online meeting (they are free); you can make the group private or public. This will provide you with a place to post notices about upcoming calls, call in information, etc. People can also post updates on a Facebook group between calls on how they are doing – whether they are in a live or virtual Joy group. It's a great way to give and receive support.

Facebook is so awesome for doing very niched community building. (There is a lot of material online about how to promote Facebook pages and groups within niches, etc.. Just Google it.) Given that there are now more than 1 billion – yes, you read that right – users on Facebook, chances are that if you put a small amount of effort into this, you'll get a a group going without too much effort.

Each member of your Joy Group should have a copy of this book, which can be used on a chapter-by-chapter basis to prod discussion or bring up issues to work on each week. Please respect the copyright protection on this material and do not share copies of the book illegally. Many thanks.

Joy Groups can morph and manifest themselves in many ways, so the key to running a successful one is to stay loose and allow the group to create itself and change as it needs to.

Who Gets to Run the Joy Group?

As long as there is someone to rally the troops and make a few phone calls, really supportive Joy Groups tend to run themselves. While it is important there be one person to set up the logistics of the group and serve as its central contact, most major decisions should be made collectively by the group, itself. Being the key contact person can be a rotating job within the group.

At the first meeting, the group should decide how often to meet and where, and (very importantly) whether to include food or not. Virtual Joy Groupers can meet over lunch at their desk if that works – the mute button is handy here. Together, the group should choose how much of the book to use in this work, and how much time to devote to each member's progress reports. Most of all, the group should understand their terrifically important role as dream-nudgers and supporters, and do their best to protect and nurture their group as a whole.

Each Joy Group will have its own particular character, and the job of its members is to express that quality. One group of writers I was in always met in slightly seedy New York bars with checkered tablecloths and decent burgers. Drinking beers and chewing the fat over "the business" was really important to our little group. Yet, another support group I was in always wanted to meet in light-filled public places, where we sipped decaf coffee, bared our souls, and closed each meeting with a prayer. Both groups worked because they reflected exactly what the people in the group wanted and needed.

What Does a Joy Group Do, Exactly?

Support each other, of course, which usually requires breaking the ice. If you meet live, you might want to do this by having everyone come to the first meeting with a 'no-name tag'. This is a name tag you make for yourself that expresses your essence without using your name. It doesn't have to be a sticky, white rectangle or even a tag at all, but it does have to express what is unique about you, and it does have to be comfortably wearable throughout the session. Virtual meetings can have do a 'Verbal No Name Tag' in which everyone share something about themselves that is unique. You could spend that first meeting by having everyone present their 'no name tags' to the group and state their dreams. Then you could decide the details of how the group will work.

After that, each meeting's agenda is up to you. Discussing a chapter or an idea from the book at the beginning of each session provides a nice bit of grounding. You might use the exercises at the end of each chapter as homework, or you might not. A different person in the group can make these choices each week, or you can decide as a group how you wish to proceed. (At the end of this chapter, I added a sample Joy Group meeting agenda, which you may use or throw out altogether.)

If you do decide to discuss a different chapter each week, look for ways that its central themes show up in your life unexpectedly. For instance, if the group decides to read and discuss the chapter "Proof That Rejection Won't Kill You", don't be at all surprised if some rejection comes your way that week. Consider this your opportunity to observe, firsthand, just how you handle it.

The bulk of your support group session time should go towards the support of each other's dreams. Each member should get a chance to fill the group in on their progress since the last meeting. It helps if these updates are timed, so each person gets an equal opportunity, but this isn't absolutely necessary. The art of good listening should be practiced by the group while each member is sharing, which includes not interrupting when someone else is speaking. Also, the group should adhere to that old dictum from Twelve Step meetings: you're not there to 'fix' anyone, save anyone, or psychoanalyze their problems. Whatever frame of mind Joy Group members show up in is perfectly fine, as long as name-calling and chair-throwing don't ensue. All shares are valid, whether miserable or euphoric, and it is the job of the group to lend thoughtful, solid support but not therapy.

In other words, offering reassurance is okay, but playing shrink is not. If Mary says, "I'm kind of bummed today. So and so just said my marketing plan stinks," an appropriate response would not be "Mary, I think you're avoiding the core of your pain. Have you tried pounding some pillows?" A better response might be to empathize – "Mary, I think I know just what you're going through. Rejection *is* hell." Joy Groups are a good place to bring your suffering, because this is where you'll find supportive friends who understand.

The same goes for criticism. Our goal here is not to be John Simon, and be ruthlessly critical of all work discussed in order to be "helpful" in some misguided way. We don't listen to someone's idea for a new kind of ice cream cone, and say, "Yes, but what about the fact that extreme amounts of sugar cause cancer in lab rats?" Even if you're a paid professional, please refrain. What's sorely needed in all support groups is genuine support and encouragement, *no matter where each person is in his or her process.* We want to treat others' fragile dreams as we would like our own to be treated: with care and respect. What we want to say is something supportive like,

"Great idea for an ice cream flavor! I've never heard that one before." We want to look for the things that really work about each other's ideas. This is how everyone's ideas, including our own, get to blossom.

In any Joy Group, there is only one rule I'd insist on, and it is this: at the end of every meeting, each support group member must clearly state what he or she will do before the next meeting – and then be held accountable for it. Please write your promises down so you don't forget, and then do yourself a favor and make them happen. If you find it hard to keep your promises, try to find out why. Do you tend to overpromise? If so, it's okay to make smaller promises. Is your time cluttered up with other demands? Maybe you need to let go of other things and make your dream a bigger priority. Or are you simply succumbing to couch-potato-itis? Here is an excellent opportunity to really get clear on why you're not fulfilling your dream, and then do something tangible about it.

It is the job of the group to remember your promises from week to week, and provide support so you can fulfill them. It might be helpful to keep a running log of these promises in a notebook; someone could be appointed at each meeting to write them all down, and then bring the notebook to the next meeting. The point is not to put a lot of pressure on members of the group, but to set goals in a clean way.

No one's keeping score here, and your Joy Group is not a competitive playing field. No one is "wrong" if he can't keep his promises. Each member will be learning about herself, and her ability to follow through and be compassionate, for true support requires gentle but steadfast honesty. If someone is chronically unable to keep her promises, the group (who can certainly empathize) should not be afraid to point this out. Such difficulties are merely human, and simply need some examination and sorting out. They are also opportunities for the group, as a whole, to learn.

A Joy Group is a place where you and your dreams will be taken seriously and held with proper respect. Remember, this is God's work you're doing here, and it is the purpose of a Joy Group to support that.

At the end of the first meeting, members might want to exchange telephone numbers or email addresses to provide or get support during the ensuing week(s) – or you may wish to institute the online support platform mentioned above. You might want to close your meeting with a prayer, a pep talk, a cheer, or even potluck. Or you might simply want to say good-bye.

It's all entirely, gloriously up to you. I only ask that you make your support group as fun and freeing, and as supportive, as you possibly can.

How Often Should the Group Meet?

If it were up to me, I'd say support groups should meet every week. That's how one puts dreams in serious motion. On the other hand, if you don't feel the need to progress so fast, by all means meet less frequently.

For those of you who claim you "really do want to meet regularly but you're just too busy", again I say check out your priorities. What exactly *is* sucking up all your time? Is it something that will improve your life in the long run, or is it just that your dream is a bit intimidating to dig into? Perhaps re-reading the book would be helpful here.

Finally, whether you meet once a week or once a month, don't blow off your meetings. Your Joy Group will only work if everyone is clear in his or her commitment to show up reliably. Those who attend sporadically need to examine whether they really want to be in the group or not – and whether they really want to make their dreams happen. After all, these meeting are about your soul, so treat them with respect.

How Big Should the Group Be?

It depends entirely on the format of the meeting. If you prefer a smaller group, and want to meet for ninety minutes, then limit the group to four or five people. That way, you each get ten or fifteen minutes for progress reports with some time left over to discuss ideas and issues from the book.

On the other hand, maybe you'd like to start a much larger group at your church, or in your community. If you've got a large enough meeting space, you can have a different person facilitate the meeting each week, pick a topic, discuss it as a group, and then have a chunk of time for sharing at the end. Not everyone may get a chance to share, but the quality of the shares will undoubtedly ring bells for others in the room. This is how 12-Step groups have operated successfully for decades. And in this way, your group can truly be unlimited in size.

Be open to changing the guidelines of your group as its members naturally ebb and flow. Any size if the perfect size for a Joy Group, as long as it continues to meet your needs and move you along on the path of your dreams.

Why Does This All Sound So Unstructured?

Because it is.

Believe it or not, you are far more capable of creating exactly the type of group you want and need than I am. In order for you to have any real commitment to this group, you, yourselves, must create it first. If this sounds intimidating, relax. These guidelines are driven by the same engine that drives the book – an innate faith in your own creative process, and the knowledge that God is already supporting your dreams, whether you know it or not. Your Joy Group will undoubtedly grow and flourish exactly as it is intended to.

By creating a Joy Group, you are not only doing something extraordinarily kind for yourself, you are supporting the world at large, and that is the best part of all. In this way, you not only get to achieve your dreams, you get to see others flourish as well.

So go forth and conquer, and while you're at it, give birth to a raft of new dreams.

Sample Agenda for a Joy Group Meeting

(For use only if you feel like it. The agenda that follows is for a typical meeting once the group has gotten established.)

The group gathers. And after the necessary milling around, small talk, and general all-round greeting that goes on .. or virtual hello's if you're meeting online .. the meeting begins.

1. Some sort of opening ritual (optional)

A member (appointed at the last meeting) shares something with the group that they find to be inspiring – a quote, a poem, a story, a news item, a song, etc.. Or perhaps the group shares a prayer. On the other hand, maybe you all huddle, cheer, and then order a drink.

2. A pre-selected topic from the book is discussed.

The same person who opened the meeting, chooses something in the book they'd like to discuss– an issue or an idea, or even an exercise. They might share some personal experience they've had that's relevant, and the group, in turn, shares their own related experiences and comments.

3. Updates on dreams

Each person reminds the group what his or her promise was to do from the last meeting, regarding their dream. (Check the notebook where promises were logged for this.) Then they update the group on their progress to date. The group offers support, ideas, etceteras.

4. Promises are made for the next meeting.

Each person makes a promise of what they will accomplish by the next meeting, which is logged into a notebook by the member who will bring this notebook to the next meeting.

5. Member is chosen who will open the next meeting.

The date and location for the next meeting are chosen – anyone who knows they can't attend (for some incredibly good reason) says so now.

6. Some sort of closing ritual (also optional)

More huddles, more cheers, more prayers and exaltations. Do whatever it is that sends you off into the night (or day) with the necessary spark in your spirit.

A Final, Important Word About Joy Groups

Here is one last thing to consider before you go leaping off to start your Joy Group:

If you are a woman, think about having a group exclusively for women.

If you are a man, think about making it only for men.

There is tremendous power and a certain freedom of expression present when we get together with members of our own sex. And this isn't just because we women feel we can finally pull up our panty hose in front of each other, or because you guys can finally get down and dirty about the

Knicks versus the Bulls. It has to do with connecting on a deep, personal level, which must be present for any Joy Group to truly do its stuff.

Now this is not to say you *must* start a women's or a men's Joy Group. If you live in a less populated area, or you simply have a lot of friends of the opposite sex you want to have in your group, then by all means disregard what I'm suggesting. On the other hand, if you can arrange things by gender, do it. We should all have one corner of our lives where we can connect with our own sex, and our behavior and choices are not affected even the tiniest bit by the gender of those present.

I had the great privilege of attending a women's college, and I know this to be true. There is just something so rich, and comforting, when women – or men– get together as a group. This is why the Bulletin Boards on my web site (howmuchjoy.com) are set up so men can find each other to start men's Joy Groups, and women can start Joy Groups for women.

I believe the power we draw from our own 'sisters' or 'brothers' can truly help move us towards action.

Did you enjoy this book? Join our Advance Reader team!
To get advance looks at Suzanne's books as she writes them, join our Advance Reader team ... We'll send you coupons, samples, gifts, and even ask for feedback along the way as we publish more books.
Go to suzannefalter.com/advancereader
Read Suzanne's other work about Joy ... Surrendering to Joy

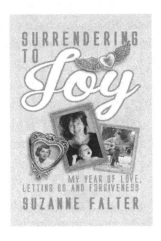

"This is one of the most remarkable books you'll read this year – or any year." – Publisher's Daily Reviews
Here's a free taster ...

An Extraordinary Gift For Us All

‿❧ August 22, 2012. Written the day after Teal died.

HERE'S TO OUR beautiful Teal, one of the most vibrant, free-spirited souls I will ever know. Teal, I was so blessed to know you in this lifetime. Your compassion, courage and plain old sense of fun were extraordinary. And to be your mother – well, that was just an amazing, amazing privilege. I am so proud of you!

Every day of our lives together I learned something about life, love and how to be a better person from Teal. (I can still hear her saying, "Mom, PLEASE don't interrupt!") Her pace was a little slower than mine, and her sensitivity toward others was absolute. She literally guided me on how to move through the world with more grace, sensitivity, and far deeper loving kindness.

What a great thing to learn from your child.

When she passed away last night, about six hours after we took her off life support, so many nurses came to us with tears in their eyes. They were so moved by Teal. Even the chief of neurology welled up as he told us what an "amazing family" we are. We felt it and continue to feel it. That has a lot to do with Teal's deep desire for peace and love as she walked through this world.

And so she speaks to me still. In fact, there is something Teal calls "the unified field of love". It is the urge we have now to come together in grief, comfort, Spirit and trying to understand. There is only one message, according to Teal. And that is Love and Happiness.

Going through Teal's end of life – from the call that she had suffered cardiac arrest and was in critical condition to her final hours and the decision to donate her organs – was the most profoundly spiritual experience I have ever had.

Friends from all over the world have shown up after hearing the news, reaching out to us with love and compassion. And the three of us – Teal's dad and her brother and I – have truly appreciated the outreach.

So I am not suffering as much as you'd think right now. Instead, I feel a profound sense of peace and even gratitude for this experience, with occasional bursts of sobbing and grief.

The ground of being now is one of love – for what else can one take from this?

More on Self-Care from Suzanne

You'll find more of Suzanne's special brand of self-care in her free **Self-Care Resource Library**. It's yours in a click at suzannefalter.com/freeresources.

Suzanne's healing podcast, **The Self-Care Soother**, helps you slow down and relax. You'll also hear from current experts about all kinds of self-care. You can find it on your smart phone's Podcast app, iTunes, Spotify and most podcast directories.

Suzanne's quick and easy online course, **Self-Care for Extremely Busy Women**, helps you focus on your own self-care and make a powerful plan in under two hours. Find it at suzannefalter.com/selfcare.

Suzanne would also love to have you in her **Self-Care Group for Extremely Busy Women** on Facebook. Just type Self-Care into Groups on Facebook and join us!

Finally, would you consider leaving a review of *How Much Joy Can You Stand* on Amazon?

We would be highly grateful.

Also by Suzanne Falter

All titles are available in audiobook, ebook and paperback.

NON-FICTION
The Extremely Busy Women's Guide to Self-Care:
Do Less, Achieve More, and Live the Life You Want

Surrendering to Joy:
My Year of Love, Letting Go and Forgiveness

The Joy of Letting Go:
Encouraging Thoughts for Challenging Times

FICTION
The Oaktown Girls series
Driven
Committed
Destined

The Transformed series
(with co-author Jack Harvey)
Transformed: San Francisco
Transformed: Paris
Transformed: POTUS

About the Author

Suzanne Falter is an author, speaker, blogger and podcaster who has published both fiction and non-fiction, as well as essays. She also writes and speaks about self-care and the transformational healing of crisis, especially in her own life after the death of her daughter Teal.

Suzanne's essays have appeared in *O Magazine*, *The New York Times*, *Elephant Journal*, *Tiny Buddha* and *Thrive Global* among others. Her fiction titles include the *Oaktown Girls* series of lesbian romances, and the romantic suspense series, *Transformed*.

Suzanne is also the host of podcasts The Self-Care Soother and Before the Afterlife. Her non-fiction work, blog, podcasts and her online course, Self-Care for Extremely Busy Women, can be found at www.suzannefalter.com and on Facebook, Twitter, YouTube, and Pinterest.

She lives with her wife in the San Francisco Bay Area.

Acknowledgments

I wish my great production team on this project, including our cover artist, Tim Barber at DISSECT DESIGNS and our excellent formatter, Maureen Cutajar. Audio engineering of our audiobook was done by Tim Hallowell and the Podcasting Group.

—SVF

CPSIA information can be obtained
at www.ICGtesting.com
Printed in the USA
BVHW030658240721
612788BV00004B/68